Catholic Spirituality and Prayer in the Secular City

Robert A. Burns

UNIVERSITY PRESS OF AMERICA,® INC.
Lanham • Boulder • New York • Toronto • Plymouth, UK

Copyright © 2008 by
University Press of America,® Inc.
4501 Forbes Boulevard
Suite 200
Lanham, Maryland 20706
UPA Acquisitions Department (301) 459-3366

Estover Road
Plymouth PL6 7PY
United Kingdom

Library of Congress Control Number: 2008927393
ISBN-13: 978-0-7618-4127-2 (clothbound : alk. paper)
ISBN-10: 0-7618-4127-X (clothbound : alk. paper)
ISBN-13: 978-0-7618-4128-9 (paperback : alk. paper)
ISBN-10: 0-7618-4128-8 (paperback : alk. paper)
eISBN-13: 978-0-7618-4190-6
eISBN-10: 0-7618-4190-3

Contents

Introduction

Much has changed in the world since the decade of the 1960s. The United States has become the most religiously pluralistic nation that has ever existed. The great majority of Americans believe in God or a higher power. On the other hand, the contemporary world embraces an image of a secularized society. Sacral forms of society have been torn down. In effect, secularization is the process by which a society strips itself of the religious ideas, beliefs, and institutions that once governed its life in order to make itself autonomous, that is, to find within itself and solely by reference to itself, the methods, structures and laws of societal living.

The process of secularization was supported at the Second Vatican Council. In the *Pastoral Constitution on the Church in the Modern World.* We read:

> If by the autonomy of earthly affairs we mean that created things and societies themselves enjoy their own laws and values which must be gradually deciphered, put to use, and regulated by men, then it is entirely right to demand that autonomy. Such is not merely required by modern man, but harmonizes also with the will of the Creator. For by the very circumstances of their having been created, all things are endowed with their own stability, truth, goodness, proper laws, and order (no. 36).

This autonomy is not in contradiction to Church teaching but rather is seen in tandem with such teaching. However, if God is eliminated from this equation, secularism results. Secularism believes that there is nothing beyond the world as we know it. The Church seeks to bridge the gap between secularism and faith as is evidenced in the *Pastoral Constitution on the Church in the Modern World*. It seeks to promote Christian values in society, not accepting the value of the world uncritically.

In the United States, against the background of secularization, the religious atmosphere has changed radically in the past 40 years. In 1965 President Lyndon Johnson signed the Immigration and Naturalization Act which opened the door to immigrants from all over the world. As a result approximately one million immigrants legally enter the United States each year. They bring with them their religious traditions such as Islam, Buddhism, Hinduism and many others. The religious scenario is rapidly changing.

Within this diversified religious and secularized world Catholics as always are called upon to develop their spiritual lives. Secularization implies the removal of the religious norm from everyday activities and it affects Catholics as it does all members of our society. The task of the Church is to re-establish the link between faith and life; in other words, to reconstruct Catholic spirituality.

Chapter One, "The New Religious America," analyzes religious pluralism in the United States as well as the challenges to spiritual practice which have occurred because of recent societal changes.

Chapter Two, "Spirituality Today," deals with the question of the meaning of spirituality and the various approaches Catholics are taking to develop their spiritual lives.

Chapter Three, "Catholic Mystics and Spiritual Writers," presents a brief examination of spiritual leaders of the past and present, male and female, who offer great examples and teachings about spirituality and prayer.

Chapter Four, "Lay Spirituality and Prayer," considers the priesthood of all the faithful and their common call to holiness. The example and teaching of Jesus regarding prayer and the role of the Mass, the sacraments and contemplation are discussed.

Chapter Five, "Catholic Feminist Theology and Spirituality," presents the feminist critique of Catholic theology and worship as well as suggestions by several prominent female writers as to how the Church can improve its teaching in regard to female spirituality. The question of ministry, including the ordination of women to the priesthood, is also discussed.

Chapter Six, "Hispanic Theology and Spirituality in the United States," deals with the needs of Hispanics and how they can be met. In order to preserve the richness of their spiritual life and cultural values, pastoral strategies are discussed. As will be seen, the American bishops have been very supportive in addressing the needs of Hispanics but there is still a long way to go in many parishes, for a variety of reasons.

Chapter Seven, "African-American Theology and Spirituality," deals, first of all, with African Spirituality and its characteristics. Following this the pastoral letter of the ten Black Catholic bishops, *What We Have Seen and Heard* (1984), suggests four major gifts which Black Catholics have and should share within the Black community at large and within the Church. Finally, the liturgical adaptations to Black culture, the role of music and the features of Black Catholic theology are discussed.

Chapter Eight, "Devotional Catholicism," presents a brief history of Catholic devotional practices in the United States and the demise of many of these activities when modern languages replaced the use of Latin and the laity were encouraged to participate in the liturgy. The recent resurgence of devotional practices and the reason for this complete the chapter.

Chapter Nine, "'Spiritual,' but not 'Religious,'" examines those who find participation in religious organizations stifling, those who are "unchurched." Approximately 38 percent of the American population belongs in this category. In this regard the "New Age" movement is discussed. Finally, the efforts of many Catholic parishes and the programs they are offering in guiding those who are seeking a deeper spirituality complete the chapter.

Hopefully the brief analyses found in this book will enable the reader to see him/herself in a proper context and provide an avenue or avenues for a deeper spirituality.

Chapter One

The New Religious America

Diana Eck in her mind-opening book *The New Religious America* describes the radical changes in the landscape of religion in America beginning in 1965. The subtitle of her book is instructive, namely, "How a Christian Country Has Now Become the World's Most Religiously Diverse Nation."[1] The changes have been gradual and yet monumental, but so gradual that most Americans are not aware of what has been taking place.

In 1965 President Lyndon Johnson signed the Immigration and Naturalization Act at the base of the Statue of Liberty, which opened the doors to immigrants from all over the world. The legislation came in the wake of the Civil Rights Act, passed in 1964. As a result of the new legislation approximately one million immigrants legally enter the United States each year, including many from Asian countries. The admittance of Asians is noteworthy since, with the exception of Filipinos, Asians had not been allowed to enter the United States, nor had they been allowed citizenship, since 1924. In that year the Johnson-Reed Act of Congress effectively disallowed new immigration from outside Western Europe. Quotas were established on the basis of national origin based on the 1890 census. In 1923, the Supreme Court had ruled that Asians were ineligible for citizenship according to a 1790 Congressional statute that limited citizenship to the "white race."

According to Dr. Eck, the percentage of foreign-born Americans is greater today than ever before, even than during the peak of immigration 100 years ago. The fastest growing groups are Asians and Hispanics. Between 1990 and 1999 the Asian population grew 43 percent, to 10.8 million. And by 2002 the number increased to about 12 million. Hispanics between 1990 and 1999 increased by 38.8 percent, to 31.3 million and as of 2002 numbered more than 35.3 million. (Incidentally, that same year the African-American population rose to 36.4 million.)

With the arrival of immigrants from all over the world and not simply from Western Europe, the religious scenario began to change. Immigrants brought their religious traditions with them such as Islam, Buddhism, Hinduism and those of Jain, Sikh, Zoroaster and others. Today, for example, there are more U. S. citizens who are Muslim than Episcopalians or Presbyterians and as many Muslims as Jews. Add to this the fact that immigrants from Cuba and Haiti have brought Afro-Caribbean traditions, blending African and Catholic symbols and images. And recent Jewish immigrants from Russia and the Ukraine have added to the internal diversity of American Judaism.

However, it is probably safe to say that most Christian, Jewish or secular Americans have never visited a mosque or a Hindu or Buddhist temple, let alone have any real understanding of the basic teachings of those and other religious traditions, and unfortunately, have rather weak understanding of their own traditions.

In 1955 Will Herberg, a noted sociologist, published a well-received book, *Protestant, Catholic, Jew*.[2] He did not examine African-American churches, Native American religions, Buddhism, Hinduism or a raft of other religions. This was due in great measure to the exclusion of new immigrants following the 1924 legislation. The American scene had not been broadened in 1955. Herberg argued that post-World War II America was a "triple melting pot" in which Protestants tended to marry Protestants, Catholics tended to marry Catholics, and Jews tended to marry Jews. Religion had taken the place of ethnicity as the "differentiating element" in American life. Herberg wrote:

> The newcomer is expected to change many things about him as he becomes an American—nationality, language, culture. One thing, however, he is not expected to change—and that is his religion. And so it is religion that with the third generation has become the differentiating element and the context of self-identification and social location.[3]

He argues that by the third generation people had lost the language and culture of their grandparents but had retained their religion. He adds that by and large, "to be an American today means to be either a Protestant, Catholic, or a Jew."[4]

When Herberg's analysis was presented the dominance of Protestantism in America was nearing its end. In 1960 John F. Kennedy, a Catholic, was elected president of the United States, and his administration included many Jewish appointees. Also, after 1965, only 10 years after publication of Herberg's book, many new religious voices began to appear. A new era of religious pluralism was inaugurated.

Diana Eck argues that *"pluralism* is not just another word for diversity. It goes beyond mere plurality or diversity to active engagement with that plurality . . . diversity alone is not pluralism. Pluralism is not a given but must be created. Pluralism requires participation and attunement to the life and energies of one another."[5] In other words, an effort must be made to attain a constructive understanding of one another. And although tolerance is much better than intolerance, it is not enough. It can create a climate of restraint but not of understanding. It can also beget a rather elitist attitude. Here is the problem. The Gallup polls indicate a rather low level of religious literacy among Americans, even in regard to one's own community. It will be a challenge to the various religious groups to overcome this lack of knowledge. And it is noteworthy that Religious Studies departments in colleges and universities throughout the country are flourishing and working toward such a constructive understanding. Hopefully more and more seminaries will also require basic literacy in the world religions as part of their training and offer courses on world religions to their congregations.

Pluralism is not relativism. It does not eliminate deep commitments to one's own religious traditions or secular commitments. Encounters with persons of other faiths can give one a broader and clearer understanding of one's own faith. Such dialogue must be based not only on commonalities, but on the significance of real differences. For example, the *Decree on Ecumenism* issued at the Second Vatican Council informs Roman Catholics that from such dialogue with other Christians there will emerge still more clearly what the position of the Catholic Church is. In this way, too, [the decree continues] we will better understand the attitude of our separated brethren.[6] A deeper understanding of one's Christian faith can also emerge from dialogue with members of other religions such as Judaism, Islam and Buddhism, to name but a few. The dialogue with Judaism has been and continues to be rewarding to all involved and a dialogue with Islam has begun. A significant Christian-Buddhist dialogue has also emerged. Thomas Merton helped to promote this dialogue. Merton, a Trappist monk who lived in the Gethsemani Abbey in Kentucky, engaged in a spiritual dialogue with Buddhists personally and through correspondence. He, along with other Christians, found they were enriched by various forms of Buddhist meditation practice. In 1968 Merton was given permission to leave his abbey and travel to Asia where he met the Dalai Lama. Unfortunately, Merton died in an untimely fashion when he was accidentally electrocuted in his hotel room in Thailand. Merton's influence will be discussed in a later chapter.

In the United States, beginning in the 1960s, fundamentalist Christian groups, later spurred on by the Moral Majority and the Christian Coalition, among others, coupled with the messages of an assortment of television evangelists, have stressed the idea of a "Christian America," often with little awareness of the new pluralistic religious scenario in the United States. In fact, the United States has become the most religiously diverse nation in history. It remains to be seen whether or not we will be able to work together despite religious diversity. This will in great measure depend on our efforts to actually know one another.

Besides the great variety of religions other changes have occurred in the past 50 years in attitudes toward organized religion. Although churches, synagogues, mosques and temples are still faring very well, the impact of "religion" has radically changed for many. The meaning of "spirituality" seems to be moving in new directions. For many these beliefs are becoming more eclectic and their faith commitments are more private. Robert Wuthnow in his excellent book *After Heaven: Spirituality in America Since the 1950s* defines spirituality as follows:

> At its core spirituality consists of all the beliefs and activities by which individuals attempt to relate their lives to God or to a divine being or some other conception of a transcendent reality.[7]

It seems clear that spirituality in the past 50 years or so has changed, and in many ways has stayed the same. Many Americans say they are spiritual but not religious, i.e., they don't belong to an organized religion. This marks quite a change in the American scene since at the beginning of the 20th century virtually all Americans practiced their faith within a Jewish or Christian framework. At that time, as Wuthnow writes: "Organized religion dominated their experience of spirituality, especially when it was reinforced by ethnic loyalties and expressed in family rituals."[8] Such patterns maintained through the decade of the 1950s, but profound changes began to occur beginning in the 1960s. These changes were brought about by an increasingly complex social and cultural environment. In the past most people lived in basically stable and geographically confined communities. This began to change in the 1950s and 1960s. Today's society is much more mobile and is also confronted with secularity. As a result, some are searching in a variety of ways to rediscover the sacred and to deepen their spiritual lives. Others continue to understand the sacred in traditional ways. In other words, traditional religious practice remains appealing to many while others are looking elsewhere.

Prior to the decade of the 1960s, one's home was generally understood as an extension of the church or synagogue. This was reinforced with the use of the Bible, religious pictures and statues and the practice of various devotions. The spirituality that was practiced was habitual and defined the core of one's being so basically that little thought needed to be given to these routines and rituals. In the Catholic Church, devotionalism was carefully regulated by the hierarchy. Prayers printed in devotional guidebooks were officially approved and many were associated with congregational worship, such as novenas and the Stations of the Cross. Popular spirituality in the 1950s was also closely identified with prominent religious figures, notably, for Catholics, Bishop Fulton Sheen. In Protestant circles members of the various churches were attuned to preachers such as Rev. Billy Graham. And in the social sciences, leading scholars of religion in the United States such as Joseph Fichter, Thomas O'Dea and Peter Berger were church members or priests interested chiefly in the well-being of religious institutions. These individuals helped to fortify the importance of organized religion. In the 1950s spirituality was basically tied to participation in a local congregation. It is worth noting that in the 19th century less than half of the population belonged to a church or synagogue, but in the 1950s at least three-fourths of the American population were members of these communities.[9] A Gallup poll conducted in 1956 put the number at 80 percent.

The decade of the 1960s, which was very turbulent, had a dramatic impact on American spirituality. Many began to adopt an eclectic style of spirituality. Middle-class definitions of who God is or where God could be found were questioned, which led to uncertainty as to how one could be in touch with the sacred. Many arrived at the notion that God could be found in ways they had never imagined, often outside the sphere of organized religion. They were inspired by the Civil Rights movement, the African-American traditions, increased knowledge of world religions, rock music, contemporary art, and the feminist movement. And the Vietnam War made many aware of the problem of evil. Underground churches appeared seeking to meet the needs of the time. For many the Civil Rights movement led them to the conclusion that diversity is good and personal exploration of values was desirable. Drive-in churches began to appear and as Robert Wuthnow writes:

> . . . clergy shortened sermons to accommodate the time demands of their parishioners, religious bookstores began to appear, the bookstore chains that developed in shopping malls started to carry Bibles and inspirational books and college campuses started to provide tracts and sign-up sheets for religious organizations as a cafeteria-style approach to promoting religious interests along with other student activities.[10]

One of the most significant aspects of the 1960s was the fact that many began to see that spirituality and organized religion might be separate entities. College training brought about exposure to new ideas and information. Also, society became ever more mobile and as one moved away from home, family, and community ties. There was an increased propensity toward eclecticism in one's attitudes and activities. For example, the number of young women on campuses tripled during the 1960s, and they were certainly influenced by the changes which were occurring, as were their male counterparts. Whereas their mothers, for the most part, spent their twenties at home raising small children, young women were now living in dormitories or apartments studying or establishing their careers in business. Exposure to new ideas helped bring about enormous changes in lifestyle and attending college was one of the major sources of such change.

In the decade of the 1960s, college enrollments jumped from 3.6 million to 8.6 million students. Due to the prosperity of the period many Americans were able to take advantage of the new opportunities which were available to them. Not only were new religions introduced in the 1960s which encouraged Americans to be more eclectic in their spirituality, but the nature of freedom was also redefined. The notion of freedom which emerged often proved to be unstable since freedom became a matter of subjective opinion and choice. At times one had no real parameters in decision-making.

By the decade of the 1970s Americans had to think hard about what it meant to be spiritual. Some began to look to Eastern spirituality. In the United States the practice of Zen Buddhism, Transcendental Meditation and other Asian spiritual practices became more common. The practitioners were generally young, single or divorced, relatively well-educated and living in urban areas. At the same time feminist spirituality continued to develop. Great stress was placed on egalitarianism and cooperative social relationships including the right of women to participate equally in religious services and institutions. Religious symbols were severed from automatic connections with their meanings because their patriarchal imagery was being questioned. It became increasingly difficult for many Americans to remain in their congregations because of the many changes which were taking place.

During the 1970s personal discipline was emphasized to curb the excesses of the 1960s. A number of parents took their children out of public schools and homeschooled them, inculcating the moral and spiritual discipline they felt was needed, together with great stress on a good education. The stress on the need for spiritual discipline increased in the 1980s. Television preachers such as Billy Graham, Jerry Falwell and Pat Robertson continually stressed the need to return to strict biblical standards of moral and spiritual discipline. Falwell, the founder of the Moral Majority movement, especially drew attention to pornography, violence on television and abortion.[11]

Pat Robertson, who organized the influential conservative movement known as the Christian Coalition, warned that the United States would go into a dramatic tailspin if spiritual discipline was not recovered.[12] The experimental "Jesus People" of the 1960s were gradually replaced by groups such as Campus Crusade for Christ, Intervarsity Fellowship, charismatic Catholics, and others. Although conservative Protestantism became one of the major vehicles for emphasizing spiritual and moral discipline, mainstream Catholic and Protestant leaders also stressed such discipline.

Despite the emphasis on discipline in the 1980s, great changes at the spiritual level did not take place in the lives of most Americans. Regarding such discipline, Robert Wuthnow writes:

> . . . research shows that Americans who favored it—even those who followed it in their religious lives—did not abandon the commitment to freedom that had emerged in the 1960s. They did adopt positions on specific issues such as sexuality, abortion and school prayer but otherwise the desire for discipline appears to have had little impact on the way most Americans led their lives.[13]

The religious attitude for most Americans was that of a rather casual interest in spirituality. Little evidence exists of people engaged in spiritual discipline which in any way led them to abandon their standard of living or to seek a deeper relationship with God by means of prayer and meditation. Spirituality requires practice and this in turn demands a daily commitment which was often lacking. Again, to quote Wuthnow:

> To have achieved the personal and social transformation that many (on the left as well as on the right) were calling for in the 1980s would have required greater dedication and more sacrifice than ever popularly associated with the idea of discipline.[14]

During this period virtually all Americans continued to believe in God. But because of the uncertainty of the times and the disruptions of society coupled with what was for many the loss of a sacred space, interest in angels became widespread. As the noted sociologist of religion, Father Andrew Greeley, comments, "We live in a problematic and dangerous universe (and) we feel that God is a great distance from us. Angels . . . have the appeal of beings who will take care of us."[15]

The present interest in supernatural phenomena such as miracles and angels is interesting since most people place spirituality on the periphery of their daily lives. For the most part, due to their busy routines, they do not set aside portions of their day for prayer, meditation, worship, spiritual reading or service to others. Yet to practice spirituality means that one intentionally engages in activities which deepens his or her relationship to the sacred. A practice-oriented spirituality has been intrinsic to all religious traditions. Recently a number of churches have sponsored groups who study spiritual figures such as St. Augustine, St. Francis of Assisi, and St. Teresa of Avila as well as Thomas Merton, Mother Teresa and other more contemporary spiritual writers. Bible studies and prayer groups are popular as well. These efforts are being made to aid those interested in the practice of spirituality. This focus on practice helps order one's thought to the fact that spirituality can be exercised in the complex arena of contemporary society. From the writings of Thomas Merton, Henry Nouwen, Ronald Rolheiser and others, it is clear that spirituality deepens only as it is practiced and practice includes such activities as prayer, meditation and acts of service. As Joel S. Goldsmith writes, "Meditation, if practiced faithfully, opens our consciousness to permit God to function in our life—*but it must be practiced*."[16] Whatever else it might mean, it is clear that spiritual practice involves intentionally seeking contact with God and of relating one's life to the divine. To do so is not easy but it is rewarding.

Some people who are deeply committed to spiritual practices do so within their local parish and are involved in seminars, study sessions, Bible studies or prayer and meditation groups. Others practice spirituality on their own, apart from any commitment to an organized religion. Even then their practices are facilitated by some existing religious tradition or traditions. Some people who practice spirituality spend a great deal of time interacting with others, whereas others find it necessary to withdraw from such interaction in order to read, pray and meditate. But the core of a person's spirituality is his or her relationship with God. And in attempting to deepen that relationship most people emphasize the value of rooting their spiritual practice in a specific tradition, rather than having to pursue such spiritual activities in a vacuum. In doing so they know they are following practices that people have engaged in for centuries. In a later chapter we will review the contemplative traditions of Roman Catholicism. As Alistair MacIntyre, a professor of moral theology at the University of Notre Dame, observes regarding those who follow traditional spiritual practices: "to enter into a practice is to enter into a relationship not only with its contemporary practitioners, but also with those who have preceded us in the practice of its present point."[17] Jack Kornfield in *A Path with Heart: A Guide through the Perils and Promises of Spiritual Life* emphasizes the value of practicing within a single tradition (although not exclusively) over a period of time. He writes:

> If we do a little of one kind of practice and a little of another, the work we have done in one often doesn't continue to build as we change to the next. It is as if we were to dig many shallow wells instead of one deep one. In continually moving from one approach to another, we are never forced to face our own boredom, impatience and fears.[18]

So, for Roman Catholics, it is important to understand the traditions of spiritual development found in their community. People who engage in spiritual practices such as Mother Teresa, for example, emphasize how deeply interlaced these activities are with other parts of their lives. It is important to interlace specific devotional activities with other realms of human experience such as being available for others, working with the poor, dealing with illness and death, comforting the afflicted, and, generally, making a concerted effort to practice Christ's teachings. As Sister Joan Chittister observes in her book on contemplative prayer, there is a paradoxical relationship between spiritual practice and involvement in society. She writes:

> Contemplative prayer . . . is prayer that sees the whole world through incense — a holy place, a place where the sacred dwells, a place to be made different by those who pray, a place where God sweetens living with the beauty of all life. Contemplative prayer . . . unstops our ears to hear the poverty of widows, the loneliness of widowers, the cry of women, the vulnerability, the struggle of outcasts.[19]

The fact that society has changed so much in the past half century means that a heightened level of attention must be given to spiritual practice since fewer people live within defined religious communities and more options are available for those who desire to live a devout spiritual life. What must be remembered is that the purpose of spiritual practice is not to elevate an isolated set of activities over the rest of life, but rather to stimulate the spiritual impulse that animates *all of life.*

Chapter Two

Spirituality Today

In the contemporary English language few words are as misunderstood as the word spirituality. In terms of signifying what it means today, it is a relatively new word. Only in the last 30 or 40 years has this word become a part of our common vocabulary. Now bookstores, whether religious or secular, stock a great many books dealing with spirituality. In describing spirituality, Sandra Schneiders writes: " . . . virtually everyone talking about spirituality today is talking about self-transcendence which gives integrity and meaning to the whole of life and to life in its wholeness by situating and orienting the person within the horizon of ultimacy in some ongoing and transforming way."[1] She goes on to say:

> We might define Christian spirituality as that particular actualization of the capacity for self-transcendence that is constituted by the substantial gift of the Holy Spirit establishing a life-giving relationship with God in Christ within the believing community. Thus, Christian spirituality is a trinitarian, christological, and ecclesial religious experience.[2]

The transcendent, the energizing source of Christian spirituality, is fully revealed in Jesus Christ. However, it is important to note that within other religious, cultural and historical frameworks analogous experiences of the ultimate have fostered analogous life-integrating dynamics which can legitimately be called spiritualities.

People in the United States retain faith in God but that faith tends to be marginal to the rest of their lives. Belief is not a characteristic problem, but the extent to which one's understanding and behavior are guided by that belief surely is. At Vatican Council II the *Pastoral Constitution on the Church in the Modern World* states: "The split between the faith which many profess and their daily lives deserves to be counted among the more serious errors of our age."[3] The Council makes clear there is a need not only of daily prayer but also indicates that the spiritual life of a Christian requires working for the cultural, economic, social and political good of humanity. In other words, a Christian is called on to continue the creative and redemptive work of God in the world.

One of the major problems in developing a spiritual life is the process of secularization. In itself secularization does not mean the loss of faith, but the isolation of faith and religion from the rest of life. It implies the compartmentalization of life into various segments and the removal of the religious norm from everyday activities. In this regard Msgr. Philip Murnion writes:

> Secularization is not simply a process that has affected the culture 'out there'; it is a process that has affected church culture as well. Thus, church efforts to address precisely our challenge of faith must be directed not so much at shoring up doctrine and orthodoxy, however important these may be, but at reestablishing the link between faith and life, or . . . at reconstructing Catholic spirituality.[4]

Everyone has a spirituality, either a life-giving one or a destructive one. What shapes our actions is our spirituality. Spirituality deals with the way we channel our desires. As Ronald Rolheiser writes: "The disciplines and habits we choose to live by will either lead to a greater integration or disintegration in the way we are related to God, others, and the cosmic world."[5] He goes on to indicate that the opposite of being spiritual is not one who rejects God or the idea of God, "but rather is one who has no energy and has lost all zest for living. Spirituality is that aspect of life which keeps us integrated."[6]

Every generation has struggled with spirituality. There has never been a golden age. Our present culture is not conducive to developing a healthy spirituality. There are many obstacles. Rolheiser describes several key factors which have become serious obstacles to spiritual development. Although there are many things that work against interiority, he singles out as especially hurtful the following: narcissism, pragmatism, and unbridled restlessness. Narcissism means excessive self-preoccupation; pragmatism means excessive focus on work; and restlessness means "an excessive greed for experience, an overeating, not in terms of eating, but in terms of trying to drink in too much of life."[7] These factors leave one with little time for reflection and spiritual growth. Henry Nouwen in *Reaching Out: The Three Movements of the Spiritual Life* gives an excellent description of how our desire for experience and the restlessness, hostility and fantasy it generates block solitude, hospitality, and prayer in one's life.[8] He believes we are distracting ourselves into spiritual oblivion. In the United States the struggle is not with sincerity, but with spiritual direction. We are pulled in many directions and live in a world which is rich in nearly everything from a material point of view, except clarity in the area of spirituality.

In Chapter Six of the Gospel of Matthew, Jesus specifies three aspects of Christian discipleship, namely prayer, fasting and almsgiving. In regard to these pillars of Christian spirituality, Rolheiser writes:

> However, we must understand these prescriptions in the way Jesus meant them. For him, prayer meant not just private prayer, but also keeping the commandments and praying in common with others; fasting meant a wide asceticism that included within itself the asceticism demanded by living a life of joy; and almsgiving meant, among other things, justice as well as charity.[9]

For all Christians Jesus is the center of one's spiritual life. More than anyone else he is admired and revered by his followers. But what Jesus wants is not admiration but imitation. And not simple imitation (as though that were possible). As John Shea describes throughout his *Stories of Faith*, Jesus is not a law to be obeyed or a model to be imitated, but a presence to be seized and acted upon.[10] In other words, as God once acted through Jesus, so he now acts through those who are conformed to the image of Jesus and whose behavior-pattern is in imitation of him. Jerome Murphy-O'Connor summarizes this idea in a succinct fashion. He writes:

> What Christ did in and for the world of his day through his physical presence, the (Christian) community does in and for its world. . . . In order to continue to exercise his salvific function the Risen Christ must be effectively represented within the context of real existence by an authenticity which is modeled on him.[11]

Unfortunately in today's society there is an ever-growing separation between spirituality and the church. Many aren't leaving their parishes, they just aren't going to them. There are many reasons for this including a lack of spiritual leadership, but perhaps the greatest problem is indifference and a culture of indifference. However, it is important to recall that we are essentially social by nature. Our relationship with God should be consistent with our nature. To make spirituality a private effort is to reject part of our very nature. To be a member of the church does not necessarily mean we are joined to others with whom we are emotionally or ideologically compatible. Often we are involved in the church community with people who are very different from ourselves. We are called upon to transcend our differences of race, gender, language and ideology as we share our community of faith.

If spirituality is a problem for us it may be partly because community has become a problem. One must ask to what extent American Catholics have retained a communal approach to their faith and to what extent they have adopted the individualistic approach of the American culture. Catholics today have a more voluntary approach than their parents as to the manner and degree they will participate in church life, and for this reason the quality of the local parish is of great importance. Research makes clear that living one's faith depends on the support of the community. The work of the priest-sociologist Father Andrew Greeley and others indicates that support of one's spouse and family of origin or of some other important community, is critically important for the development of an active faith.[12] Greeley points out that the most important influences are local—the religious behavior of one's spouse and the quality of preaching in the parish church. A vital parish has a real sense of church community. Many of the shared factors that fostered an intense community life have dwindled, including immigrant status, low income and discrimination. As Msgr. Philip S. Murnion observes:

> Now American Catholics have become part of the communities that have acquired significance for them, communities associated with their middle-class status and income level, with the neighborhoods in which they live, or with their vocational or avocational interests. The church is no longer needed as an enclosed, protective, and exclusive community.[13]

Murnion argues that in the United States there are five basic approaches to restoring church community, namely: traditionalism, sectarianism of the left and the right, intimacy, association, and solidarity.[14] A brief description of each approach will be helpful to our study.

TRADITIONALISM

The traditionalist response to revitalizing the parish community is a return to the past and may entail the use of the *Baltimore Catechism*, the Tridentine (Latin) Mass, pious devotions of the past, and even earlier forms of church discipline. Traditionalists want religious women, for example, to wear their habits and perform the kind of ministry that they did so well before Vatican II. As Murnion observes, this view canonizes a particular period and endows it with a special authority that no other period in church history ever enjoyed. In this approach ministry again becomes a clerical preserve and the participative structures, such as parish councils, are greatly reduced in importance, if not totally eliminated.

SECTARIANISM

The sectarian response, whether of the left or right, to revitalize parish life inevitably reduces true discipleship to an elitism that sees the true church in rather narrow focus. Those on the left see themselves as a prophetic and religious remnant. They are pacifists who engage in fasts and demonstrations or risk their freedom to preserve life and promote justice. This is certainly a powerful position, but one that will never include the whole community. The sectarian of the right is given to testimony of praise rather than of prophecy. This is the community of the Spirit, the spirituality of the charismatic renewal. For them, interior renewal is the key to community revitalization. The point is to live as much as possible the new life of the spirit rather than to try to change the world. Murnion correctly observes that no parish will completely embody either of these types of sectarian community, but some parishioners will operate with their approach as the ultimate model of community. Though both groups, the prophetic and charismatic, have much to offer, they are communities of the special movement and not the model of renewal to which all members of the parish will be called.

INTIMACY

The intimacy approach to the problem of community comes from those who would try to restore relationships within the church on *intimate terms*. Murnion refers to this response as the community of the encounter weekend, groups that foster marriage encounter, teenage encounters, and renewal programs that focus on emotional relationships among the participants. The intimacy proposed is certainly valuable because it pertains to family, forgiveness, and other important needs. Some priestly renewal programs belong in this category. Although they do not specifically propose intimacy they put a premium on fraternal relationships among priests and with the bishop. Such intimacy responds well to the fragmentations of our time and the anonymity of urban culture and can be very helpful to a parish. But it can be but one aspect of parish life, because true intimacy can be achieved only with a few others.

ASSOCIATION

A fourth approach, described by Murnion, is to give up the attempt to create community altogether and to settle for the parish as an *association*. A parish is a good association if it offers a variety of useful activities for its diverse members without trying to bind them together in a common faith, a common understanding, or a common action. Delivery of services becomes prominent, and multiplicity of activity is necessary. Many of these activities and services are undertaken not only with religious conviction but within a religious context. The association model, according to Murnion, "offers efficient services and is impatient with all the passions of the traditionalists or sectarians, and all the personal involvement required for intimacy. This is the 'civilized' religion."[15] The association model forsakes the attempt to bind people together in a community and to maintain the connection among its members while respecting their diversity of interests.

SOLIDARITY

The fifth position, and the one endorsed by Murnion, is what he refers to as the *community of solidarity*. Such a congregation moves beyond the circle of intimacy and speaks to the inclusiveness of community. Jesus did not come to bind us together with those with whom we are already intimate or with whom we already share close ties. He came to bind us together with strangers. Hence Jesus' constant positioning of the Samaritan, of the stranger, is the center of the community's concern and interest.

A community of solidarity is not only an inclusive community but is also one that sees its faith as a basis of action. This community always links its beliefs and actions. Thus the Sunday liturgy becomes its central action. All are met with hospitality and joy. A community of solidarity puts a high premium on the action of God in the human community—action that sanctifies one's daily actions and makes it possible to transcend his or her limitations. Such a community places high value on respecting tradition, on linking the past with the future, on building structures for participation and action, on presenting strong theological foundations for the positions it adopts, and on recognizing the importance of authority for any enduring and authentic community. Obviously the achievement of solidarity depends on the quality of ministry. A strong parish team is needed as is excellent preaching. The challenge is to remain open to all while representing commitment to Christian discipleship. Paternalism, or clericalism, would mark the death knell of such a parish community. Such a community of solidarity must also foster smaller, more homogenous groups throughout the parish to meet the needs of all. Finally, a community of solidarity calls for a church in which everyone in every situation is treated with respect.

Even as a member of a vital parish the practice of spirituality is challenging. For older Catholics, whether liberal or conservative, it is important to let go of the church of their youth even while grieving its passage. It is important for all, young and old alike, to accept the church as it is today. The church is very much alive with the life of today and not with the life of the decades preceding Vatican II. We should bless the church of our youth and mourn its passing and accept the path on which the Holy Spirit is leading the church today. Ronald Rolheiser gives an excellent example of why it is necessary to let go of the God of our youth in order to recognize God as he walks beside us today. He discusses the famous incident in Luke's gospel where Jesus, following his resurrection, walks with two of his disciples on the road to Emmaus (Luke 14:12–14). Rolheiser writes:

> What is curious in this incident is that the disciples, the friends of Jesus, do not recognize him, even though he has been dead for only a day and a half. Why can they not recognize him? Because they are so focused on his former reality. They are so focused on their former image of him, their former understanding of him, and the way he was formerly present to them, that now they are not open to seeing him as he walks among them.[16]

As Christians it is important that we work to develop our inner spiritual life no matter what kind of parish we belong to. This will help us to accept the Church as it is today and will allow us to become more at peace with ourselves. We should attempt to create solitude—a solitude of heart. It should be remembered that solitude is not the same thing as loneliness. It is being alone, but it is being alone in such a way that our incompleteness is a source of quiet strength and not a source of anxiety or fear. Henri Nouwen, one of the most gifted spiritual writers of the 20th century, in *Reaching Out: The Three Movements of the Spiritual Life,* lists four steps which will lead one to a restful solitude. The four steps he describes are as follows:

1) Accept your pain and incompleteness;
2) Give up the idea that at some time you will meet the right person, the right situation, or the right combination of circumstances that will make you completely happy;
3) Sit still long enough for your restlessness to turn to restfulness;
4) Be aware that turning restlessness into restfulness, into peaceful solitude, is never accomplished once and for all.[17]

By slowly converting our loneliness into a deep solitude we create a space where we can commune with Christ and paradoxically with our neighbor. However, as Nouwen observes concerning the process of acquiring solitude:

> This is a very difficult task, because in our world we are constantly pulled away from our inmost self and encouraged to look for answers instead of listening to the questions. A lonely person has no inner time nor inner rest to wait and listen. He wants answers and wants them here and now. But in solitude we can pay attention to our inner self.[18]

In solitude we can become present to ourselves. There we can live, as Anne Morrow Lindbergh says, "like a child or a saint in the immediacy of the here and now."[19] There we can also become present to others. Solitude does not pull us away from our fellow human beings but instead makes real fellowship possible. The Trappist monk, Thomas Merton, understood this very well. On January 12, 1950, he wrote in his diary:

> It is in deep solitude that I find the gentleness with which I can truly love my brothers. The more solitary I am, the more affection I have for them. It is pure affection and filled with reverence for the solitude of others.[20]

Nouwen points out that the solitude that really counts is the solitude of heart which is an inner quality or attitude that does not depend on physical isolation. Solitude can be maintained and developed in the center of a large city, in the middle of a large crowd, and in the context of a very active and productive life. A person who has developed this solitude of heart is no longer disturbed by the diverging stimuli of the surrounding world but is able to perceive and understand the world from a quiet inner circle. The development of this inner sensitivity is the beginning of a spiritual life. It is important to seek after this solitude of heart since happiness does not depend on someone else but on being at peace within oneself.

The first characteristic of the spiritual life is the continuing movement from loneliness to solitude. And, as Nouwen notes, the second important characteristic is the movement by which our hostilities can be converted into hospitality, that is, rather than being envious or jealous, we create an attitude of love and acceptance. This is a difficult task because the assumption in our society is that strangers are a potential danger and it is up to them to disprove it. Because we are so competitive almost anyone, be it a colleague at work, a classmate or a relative, to list but a few examples, can lead to fear and hostility when they are experienced as a threat of some kind. Hospitality primarily means establishing an attitude of friendship and loving acceptance of others.

The movement from hostility to hospitality is a movement that determines our relationship to other people. If we maintain an attitude of fear and hostility we block positive relationships. However, we will never be totally free of all of our hostilities and as Nouwen says:

> . . . there even may be days and weeks in which our hostile feelings dominate our emotional life to such a degree that the best thing we can do is to keep distance, speak little to others and not write letters, except to ourselves. Sometimes events in our lives breed feelings of jealousy, suspicion and even desires for revenge, which need time to be healed. It is realistic to realize that although we hope to move toward hospitality, life is too complex to expect a one way direction. But when we make ourselves aware of the hospitality we have enjoyed from others and are gratified for the few moments in which we can create some

space ourselves, we may become more sensitive to our inner movements and be more able to affirm an open attitude toward our fellow human beings.[21]

The movements from loneliness to solitude and from hostility to hospitality is undergirded by prayer which leads us to the core of the spiritual life. Without prayer our solitude and hospitality easily lose their depth. But how does one pray? Many writers have articulated their experiences in prayer and have encouraged their readers to follow their example. They often give excellent instructions on how to develop an intimate relationship with God. However, the paradox of prayer is that we have to learn how to pray while we can only receive it as a gift. The spiritual writers who speak about the discipline of prayer frequently remind us that prayer is a gift of God. They make clear that we cannot truly pray by ourselves but that it is God's spirit who prays in us. As St. Paul writes in his First Letter to the Corinthians (12:3): "No one can say, 'Jesus is Lord' unless he is under the influence of the Holy Spirit." In this regard, Nouwen writes:

> We cannot force God into a relationship. God comes to us on his own initiative, and no discipline, effort, or ascetic practice can make him come. All mystics stress with an impressive unanimity that prayer is 'grace,' that is, a free gift from God.[22]

He goes on to say:

> Prayer, therefore, is God's breathing in us, by which we become part of the intimacy of God's inner life, and by which we are born anew.[23]

And though we cannot organize or manipulate God, without a discipline of prayer we cannot receive him either. It is clear that anyone who wants to live a life of prayer cannot persevere in that desire without a concrete plan. As time passes it may be necessary to make changes in direction and to explore new methods of prayer, but without such discipline the life of prayer will most likely not deepen.

In establishing guidelines for a life of prayer it is useful to examine the lives of people for whom prayer was vital to their existence. Doing so one discovers that three "rules" are almost always apparent. These "rules" involve a contemplative reading of the Bible, silence in the presence of God, and guidance from a spiritual director. Though it is at times difficult to find a spiritual director, it is possible. When asked, the person in question usually agrees to fulfill this role. The teachings of influential historical personalities provide guidance as we will see in the next chapter where we will introduce the reader, although briefly, to some of the more noteworthy spiritual thinkers.

Chapter Three

Catholic Mystics and Spiritual Writers

Christian mysticism is not radically different from spirituality or from the Christian life. In fact mysticism is rooted in baptism and the call of all Christians to enter into the divine mystery of God's presence through Holy Scriptures, the liturgy and the sacraments. It is a gift rather than the result of one's efforts. Mysticism is potentially the spiritual dimension of every Christian's life. However, it is certainly true that some Christians have more intense experiences of God and for this reason mysticism is seen as a distinct category of spirituality, though the two are interrelated.

Richard McBrien defines mysticism as "the graced transformation of consciousness that follows upon a direct or immediate experience of the presence of God leading to a deeper union with God."[1] That union does not isolate one from others or from the world. Christian mysticism insists on a connection between the experience of God as the *presence within*, and the experience of God as the presence *in others* and in the "signs of the times." In other words, the experience of God in Jesus Christ, an experience brought about by the Holy Spirit, leads to greater apostolic activity and into service of others.

McBrien points out that because mysticism is always particular and contextual two types of mysticism are found and these were first distinguished in *The Mystical Theology* written by Denys the Areopagite, known as Pseudo-Dionysius, a Syrian monk who lived at the end of the fifth and into the early sixth century.[2] The first type is the way of imagelessness, stillness, and wordlessness (the *via negativa* or "apophatic" way). The second type is the way of imagining God by use of the human imagination or in words (the *via affirmativa* or "kataphatic" way). There is no theological basis for an absolute distinction between the two approaches since God is revealed in and through words and images as well as through other visible realities and yet is always beyond them.

In discussing mystics and spiritual writers it is important to remember that there is one Spirit, but many spiritualities. As St. Paul tells us:

> Now there are a variety of gifts, but the same spirit; and there are varieties of services, but the same Lord; and there are varieties of activities, but it is the same God who activates all of them in everyone. To each is given the manifestation of the Spirit for the common good. . . . All of these are activated by one and the same spirit, who allots to each one individually just as the Spirit chooses. (1 Cor. 12:4–7, 11).

Spiritual leaders of the past, male and female, have a great deal to teach about prayer, suffering, compassion, and social justice. They provide spiritual and psychological insights into contemporary problems and conflicts as well as creative possibilities. They help people emerge from the implicit parochialism, limitations, and biases of any age, including the contemporary one. From them can be rediscovered what the church has known from its inception, namely, that all Christians are called to holiness, not just priests and nuns, but all Christians. They also remind us that we are called to center our lives on God and to discover the love and compassion of God for all creation, including ourselves.

There is no definite date or person which represents the starting point of Christian mysticism and the ensuing spiritual writing which it produced. However, it is clear that it began in North Africa during the second and third centuries. Noteworthy in this period were members of the Christian community in Alexandria, Egypt, namely Clement of Alexandria and Origen.

CLEMENT (C.150–C.215 A.D.)

Clement of Alexandria is generally considered the first author of works on mystical theology. He lived from c.150–c.215 A.D. He was born in Athens but studied and taught in Alexandria. His best known works are the *Pedagogue (The Teacher)* and *Stromateis (Miscellanies)* where he presents his ideas regarding the vision of and union with God, though he is not a systematic writer.[3]

Clement was the first writer to introduce the words "mystical" and "mystically" into Christian literature. He emphasized that God was unknowable and inexpressable, i.e., he used the apophatic approach. He was also the first to stress the twofold goal of attaining contemplation and relating that to Christian action in the community.

ORIGEN (C.185–C.254).

Origen was a student of Clement of Alexandria and succeeded him as head of the Catechetical School in Alexandria. As a youth he castrated himself (something he later regretted) when he took literally Matthew 19:12, namely: " . . . there are eunuchs who have made themselves eunuchs for the sake of the kingdom of heaven." He was a fine preacher and was involved in many ecclesiastical debates. However, his orthodoxy was often questioned, more so in the East than in the West.

Origen was an exponent of the allegorical interpretation of Scripture and studied the Bible for the secret and hidden things of God. He believed that Christianity provides a ladder for ascending to God, from purgation to illumination and to a final knowledge of God. Importantly, he wrote that the mystery of the union between the soul and God is symbolically expressed in the Song of Songs of which he was the first Christian interpreter. His commentary on this work has only been preserved in part but it is based on the claim already held by Jewish scholars that the real meaning of this ecstatic love poem is spiritual and represents the union of the soul with God. Between the 3rd and 5th centuries such Christian mysticism found a definite expression among ascetics and monks who created a particular vocabulary and orientation which helped shape Christian spirituality for years to come.

MONASTICISM (3RD TO 5TH CENTURIES

Many early Christians developed a spirituality based on the thought of Clement and Origen who emphasized a combination of ascetism and mysticism which led to the establishment of monasticism for men and women.

St. Anthony of Egypt (251–c.356) is often referred to as the creator of *anchorite monasticism*, basically the life of a Christian hermit. In the early fourth century this form of monasticism was replaced by communities of monks living together, thus overcoming the loneliness of the anchorite mode. This community orientation developed under Pachomius (290–346) and later, in the West, under St. Benedict of Nursia (c.480–c.547) in Italy. Monasteries of women developed as well during this time frame.

CAPPADOCIAN FATHERS

Christian mystical theology was developed in the fourth century most notably by the three Cappadocian Fathers, namely, Gregory of Nyssa, his brother

Basil the Great, the founder of Basilian monasticism, and Gregory of Nazianzus. Cappadocia was a region in what is today east central Turkey. Gregory of Nyssa (330–395) was the first systematic theological thinker since Origen, who died in c.254. Gregory was one of the first, if not the first, to describe the mystical life as an ascent of the soul to God, a never-ending process leading to a greater understanding of the mystery of the Godhead. He taught that mysticism is not separate from the concerns of the world. Rather, the mystical and moral, contemplative and active involvement in human affairs, must interact with each other.

ST. AUGUSTINE OF HIPPO (354–430)

Augustine's life was motivated by contemplation which led into great activity. His book *Confessions* (or as George Will argues, *Testimony*) is the first and perhaps to this day the *greatest spiritual autobiography* ever written.[4] He wrote it in his mid-forties, a short time after he had been made a bishop. The book is devotional in its orientation, mixed with information about his childhood, youth, conversion to Christianity, and the events that followed. *Confessions* blends mystical insights with personal narrative. His total surrender to God is described in Book VIII. Augustine did not write on mysticism in a systematic fashion. Rather, his insights on prayer, contemplation and mysticism are scattered throughout his writings and many of his deepest ideas are found in his sermons and commentaries on scripture, most notably in his treatment of the Pslams, the Gospels and the First Letter of John, and in his marvelous treatise entitled *The Trinity*.

MEDIEVAL MYSTICS

From the *seventh through the early 12th century* we *know very little* of mystical life. During this period Europe was experiencing the Dark Ages. But beginning in the 12th century the Middle Ages produced great mystics. Among them were St. Bernard of Clairvaux (1090–1153), Richard of St. Victor (1120–1173), St. Francis of Assisi (1181–1226), St. Bonaventure (1221–1274), Hildegard of Bingen (1098–1179), the Dominicans Meister Eckhart (1260–1327), Henry Suso (1295–1366) and St. Catherine of Siena (1347–1380), and Julian of Norwich (1342–1423). The spiritual writings of these individuals are still in print and are valuable to read. These writers were not dull nor were they confined in their thinking. St. Catherine of Siena stands as a case in point as does Julian of Norwich.

St. Catherine of Siena (1347–1380)

Catherine became a Dominican tertiary at the age of 16, which means she was a lay member of the order bound by simple vows. She was an ascetic and mystic, but also an activist who dedicated herself to the poor and sick of Siena. She also played an active part in the ecclesiastical politics of her day. For example, when the Great Schism of the papacy occurred (three men claiming to be pope) she actively supported Pope Urban VI, urging kings and bishops in many letters to support Urban as the true pope. The record of her mystical experience is found in her *Dialogue*, her dialogue with God, which she dictated, as she did in all her writings.[5] Much of this book was dictated while Catherine was in a state of ecstasy.

She dictated the *Dialogue* in the summer of 1378. This was her only spiritual work with the exception of a collection of her prayers. The *Dialogue* begins with a prologue that characterizes Catherine's spiritual orientation. She writes:

> A soul rises up restless with tremendous desire for God's honor and the salvation of souls. She has for some time exercised herself in virtue and has become accustomed to dwelling in the cell of self-knowledge in order to know better God's goodness toward her, since upon knowledge follows love. And loving she seeks to pursue truth and clothe herself in it.[6]

For Catherine the love of God is possible only through the mediation of Christ and leads to the soul's increased desire for him. It also leads her to a desire that others will follow the same path. The *Dialogue* is both a record of Catherine's journey along the path of knowledge and love and a kind of instruction for others. The goal of her journey, for herself and others, is the perfection of the Christian life which happens only when one is in union with God. She describes this union at the end of the book as a kind of self-understanding. Looking into the sea of the Godhead, the soul finds a mirror.

> This water is a mirror in which you, eternal Trinity, grant me knowledge: for when I look into this mirror, holding it in the hand of love, it shows me myself, as your creation, in you and in me through the union you have brought about of the Godhead with our humanity. This light shows you to me, and in this light I know you, highest and infinite good.[7]

Between the prologue and the conclusion Catherine describes a way that leads through various difficulties until it arrives at such union with God. She records the answers she received from God on the way to perfection. She speaks of the spiritual journey as the bridge to salvation; of the tears that accompany the progress of the soul; of the truth that must be received on the way to salvation; of the mystical body of the Church; of divine providence; and of obedience. Her conclusion contains a summary of her conversation with God and a hymn to the Trinity which ends with the following sentence:

> Clothe, clothe me with yourself, eternal Truth, so that I may run the course of this mortal life in true obedience and in the light of most holy faith. With that light I sense my soul once again becoming drunk! Thanks be to God! Amen.[8]

A constant theme throughout the *Dialogue* maintains love is the way to perfection and Jesus is the bridge that must be crossed from earth to heaven. The bridge is built on the stones of true virtue. In this regard she reflects on the Eucharist as that which provides spiritual nourishment for one's journey. Linked with this is her emphasis on the passion of Christ and her appreciation of Christ's self-sacrifice on behalf of humankind. She identified with Christ crucified and understood her own suffering (in 1375 she received the stigmata) to be joined with that of Christ in atonement for human sin.

In 1939 Catherine was declared the patron saint of Italy and in 1970 she was proclaimed a doctor of the Church.

Julian of Norwich (1342–1416)

Julian practiced ancient traditions of asceticism—"anchoritism" or a life of solitary withdrawal, mortification, and spiritual guidance. She also manifests features common to her late medieval English setting such as a deep mysticism and identification with Christ and his human suffering. Like Catherine of Siena, the passion of Christ became the object of her devotion. But she remained a hermitess and was not so much concerned about reforming the Church as she was about offering comfort to those tempted to despair of God's love and mercy.

Little is known about Julian's life. For many years she probably lived in a cell next to the church of St. Julian in Norwich, England. Wherever she had been educated she clearly was familiar with the Latin authors of the Western contemplative traditions. Her spiritual writings were composed in Middle English, in which she was an accomplished stylist.

Julian left one document, *The Showings* or *Revelations of Divine Love* which exists in two forms. The first, or the "Short Text," was written soon after she received sixteen revelations in May, 1373. The "Long Text" dates from 1393 and is the result of her continuing meditations upon her religious experience. This text represents her mature spiritual thought based on the sixteen revelations she received while in an ecstatic state.[9]

The revelations led to her teachings on divine love which she saw as the basis of all human existence. In the "Long Text," which is the basis of what follows in this discussion of her spiritual teachings, she bases her teaching on Scripture and tradition, as one of the book's final passages makes clear. She writes:

I pray almighty God that this book may not come except into the hands of those who wish to be his faithful lovers, and those who will submit themselves to the faith of Holy Church and obey the wholesome understanding and teaching of men who are of virtuous life, settled age and profound learning; for this revelation is exalted divinity and wisdom, and therefore it cannot remain with him who is a slave to sin and to the devil. And beware that you do not accept one thing which is according to your pleasure and liking, and reject another, for that is the disposition of heretics. But accept it all together, and understand it truly; it all agrees with Holy Scripture, and is founded upon it, and Jesus, our true love and light and truth, will show this to all pure souls who meekly and perseveringly ask this wisdom from him.[10]

As mentioned above, Julian focused on the passion of Christ as the medium of God's love for us, and her visions which were given in response to three petitions she had made, revealed to her the most intimate details of Christ's physical suffering. These visions grew in intensity as she experienced a serious physical illness for which she had asked in one of her petitions. In her other two petitions she asked for recollection and insight into the passion of Christ and for "three wounds" which she also received, namely, "true contrition, loving compassion, longing with my will for God."[11]

Julian was granted sixteen visions of Christ's passion which were painfully realistic and are linked with Julian's own insight into God's redemptive activity. The knowledge of the Trinity as creative Godhead, dwelling in our souls "in Christ Jesus our Creator," underlies her emphasis on the worthiness of the created world and its eventual healing. Her eschatology is one of eventual restoration, reflected in the following statement, "Sin is necessary, but all will be well, and all will be well, and every kind of thing will be well." Julian tells us she received these words from Jesus himself.[12]

For Julian human suffering is linked to the suffering of Jesus. She concentrates on the effects of the passion of Jesus and on her own voluntary imitation of his sufferings. And she understands that the suffering of Christ was changed to joy, as will be the case with human suffering. She learned through her visions that Christians who long for God must shift their attention away from self. She believes Christians should concentrate on the joy of the Trinity and understand human suffering as a prologue to this joy.

Julian used the language of motherhood when discussing the Trinity (although this terminology had already been used by William of St. Thierry).

However, her application of this term to Christ may be a reflection of her own status as spiritual "mother." Of the "mother" in the Trinity she writes:

> I saw and understood that the high might of the Trinity is our Father, and the deep wisdom of the Trinity is our Mother, and the great love of the Trinity is our Lord. . . . And furthermore I saw that the second person, who is our Mother, substantially the same beloved person, has now become our mother sensually. . . . The second person of the Trinity is our Mother in nature in our substantial creation, in whom we are founded and rooted, and he is our Mother of mercy in taking our sensuality. And as our Mother is working on us in various ways, in whom our parts are kept undivided; for in our Mother Christ we profit and increase and in mercy he reforms and restores us, and by the power of his passion, his death and his Resurrection he unites us to our substance (i.e, to our divine nature).[13]

Julian regarded her final revelation as a confirmation of the preceding fifteen revelations. In it she was tempted by a frightening encounter with a palpable devil, after which she received a vision of her own soul, in which Jesus dwelt.

Julian contrasts the horror of sin with the happiness which is ours as the recipients of divine mercy. With the certitude of one who has seen the Christ who redeemed us, she knew of his desire to be united with us. She was convinced that love, not sin, is the ultimate determinant of our existence. In both the long and short form of her book she affirms the goodness of creation, the friendship of Christ, and the solicitude of the Trinity.

The great tradition of medieval mystics came to an end with the Protestant Reformation. Among Catholics, some of the old traditions prevailed but were now adapted to the needs of a new age that made new demands on Christian life. The Catholic Counter Reformation produced responses to the Protestant reformers. A new spirituality developed in Spain and is marked by a mixture of contemplation and action.

SPANISH MYSTICS

In *post-Reformation Spain* mystical consciousness was a mixture of austerity and activity developed during a period of geographical expansion. New emphasis was placed on individual experiences and a more subjective spirituality. The *printing press* helped to disseminate the writings of mystics during this early modern period. Jesuit and Carmelite spirituality developed, each with its own characteristics.

St. Ignatius Loyola (1491–1556)

The founder of the Society of Jesus (Jesuits) wrote his *Spiritual Exercises* and revised them throughout his life.[14] They became a guide for members of his religious order, but to this day they are also used by many of the laity as a handbook of spiritual renewal. *Exercises* uses military images (dating back to Ignatius' very brief military career) and expresses *spirituality of service to others*. In fact, *Exercises* teaches a spirituality geared to Christian ministry and the tasks of daily life and yet the good expressed is a direct experience of God. The Jesuit order was instrumental in teaching Ignatian spirituality and did so by introducing spiritual practices such as *retreats* and s*piritual direction* which helped spread new forms of spirituality in early modern Europe to laity as well as to clergy.

ST. TERESA OF AVILA (1515–1582)

Although Teresa, a Carmelite nun, had no theological training, her writings are accepted as the classical exposition of the contemplative life and are still widely read. They include: her *Life, The Way of Perfection, Foundations, The Interior Castle*, and a number of letters and poems.[15] She describes how her mystical experiences developed as a result of her life of prayer. In *The Interior Castle* she describes the highest level of mystical union, the "spiritual marriage" of the soul and God, which always leads her back to an active service of God carried out by serving one's neighbor in a joyous and generous manner.

Teresan spirituality is marked by an intense devotion to Jesus, to the humanity of Christ. Much of her prayer centers on Christ as a friend and companion. On the basis of her own painful experience of years of frustration in praying, Teresa repeatedly warns against trying to bypass the humanity of Jesus in an effort to reach his divinity. Teresa defines mental prayer in terms of a friendly connection with Christ, "an intimate sharing between friends . . . taking time to be alone with Him who we know loves us."[16]

This focus is especially evident in the prayer instructions found in *The Way of Perfection* where she writes:

> As is already known, the examination of conscience, the act of contrition, and the sign of the cross must come first. Then, . . . since you are alone, strive to find a companion. Well what better companion than the Master Himself . . .? Represent the Lord Himself as close to you and behold how lovingly and humbly He is teaching you. . . . If you grow accustomed to having Him at your side, . . . you will find Him everywhere.

> . . . I'm not asking you now that you think about Him or that you draw out a
> lot of concepts or make long subtle reflections with your intellect. I'm not ask-
> ing you to do anything more than look at Him. . . .
>   . . . If you are joyful, look at Him as risen. . . . If you are experiencing trials
> or are sad, behold Him on the way to the garden. . . .
>   . . . I desire to suffer, Lord, all the trials that come to me and esteem them as
> a great good enabling me to imitate you in something. Let us walk together,
> Lord. Wherever you go, I will go; whatever you suffer, I will suffer.[17]

From such passages later commentators would develop the so-called Tere-
sian method of prayer even though Teresa never advocated a formal method.
However, her devotion to Jesus as friend and companion strikes a responsive
chord in many hearts today.

Teresa also made a great contribution to the understanding of spirituality
by her discussion of the various stages in one's spiritual journey. She maintains that the final phase of spiritual development is not found in ecstasies but
in a constant awareness of the indwelling of the Trinity in one's soul together
with the love of neighbor manifested by a total availability to that neighbor.

St. John of the Cross (1542–1591)

John of the Cross, a Carmelite priest, met Teresa of Avila shortly after his ordination to the priesthood in 1567. Teresa was 52 years old at the time and
was very influential in John's spiritual development. He wrote three famous
poems: *The Spiritual Canticle, The Dark Night,* and *The Living Flame of
Love*. His books, *The Ascent of Mt. Carmel* and *The Dark Night of the Soul*,
are commentaries on his poem, *The Dark Night*. His mystical writings are
widely published today.[18] He distinguishes two "nights of the soul," the
"night of the senses," where the sensual part of the soul is purified, and the
"night of the spirit," which he says only a few obtain, which leads to an intimate union with God. The 'dark night" is the image of one's journey of de-
tachment and purgation which consists of an active and passive purgation of
the senses and the spirit until the soul conforms completely to God's will.

In *The Dark Night of the Soul* John uses "dark night" to refer primarily to
the critical moments of transition in one's spiritual journey. We begin in the
"purgative way" with a busy style of praying often accompanied by consola-
tions which encourage us to practice the virtues. In the "passive night of
sense" we move beyond the busy conceptual prayers of beginners to a more
contemplative stance. Here we discover a much more inward awareness of
God's presence which begins to intensify (the "illuminative way" of "profi-
cients"). In this "passive night of the spirit we undergo a radical purification.
Both "passive nights" are painful according to John, the latter especially so.

Yet if we make it this far we will be brought to a stable union or "spiritual marriage" (the "unitive way" of the "perfect") in which we are able to enjoy a more or less continual awareness of the Trinity within, while remaining attentive to creation around us, in a state that John compares to that of Adam and Eve in paradise.[19] This sublime participation in the inner life of the Trinity is what John identifies as the goal of the journey, to be experienced fully in the life to come.

John of the Cross offers a consoling message for contemporary readers who are experiencing darkness, confusion, and crises of faith since he provides categories of meaning for these trials, allowing them to deal with these difficulties in a constructive manner. It also helps one to treat others compassionately since we can never fully know what struggles they are suffering. In the confusion of our times John provides a spirituality that helps us to keep our bearings. He reminds us that we already possess all that we need in Christ and therefore we can move ahead in the "darkness" without seeking security in material goods, false ideologies or religious institutions.

FRENCH SPIRITUAL WRITERS

During the 16th and 17th centuries the Catholic Church in France produced several outstanding spiritual writers who gained prominence, although they generally are not as well known as the Spanish mystics. Included in this group, and perhaps most notable, is St. Francis de Sales. Others in this period were St. Jeanne de Chantal (1572–1641), Blaise Pascal (1623–62), and Brother Lawrence (1611–91), a lay brother of the Discalced Carmelites. Here we will briefly discuss St. Francis de Sales and St. Jeanne de Chantal.

St. Francis de Sales (1567–1622)

St. Francis de Sales was ordained a priest in 1593 and in 1602 he was named bishop of Geneva, Switzerland. He left a large body of writings including works explaining Catholic doctrine as well as sermons and personal letters. Together with Jeanne de Chantal he founded the Visitation Order which was and is dedicated to prayer as well as visiting and caring for the sick and poor. In 1767 Jeanne de Chantal was declared a saint. Francis de Sales' best-known work is his *Introduction to the Devout Life* published in 1609.[20] The book is a marvelous spiritual guide for the laity rather than for those who live in the cloister. In it Francis asserts convincingly that the heights of spiritual life can be pursued without withdrawing from the world. Unlike the spiritual writers of his day, he believed in the inherent goodness of human nature and he argued

that human beings have a natural inclination to love God. This love is nurtured
and developed through prayer. In 1877 he was the first French writer to be declared a doctor of the Church. He had been declared a saint in 1665 and in
1923 Rome named him the patron saint of writers.

TWENTIETH CENTURY MYSTICS AND SPIRITUAL WRITERS

There are many mystics and spiritual writers in the modern period, women
and men, laity and clerics, Christian and non-Christian, people who are
widely known, whose writings and examples have inspired countless others.
Only a select few will be discussed in our brief analysis.

Edith Stein (1891–1942)

Edith Stein was a Roman Catholic convert from Judaism. She became a
Catholic in 1921, having been greatly influenced by reading the autobiography of St. Teresa of Avila. Edith became a Carmelite nun in 1934. By then she
had a Ph.D. in philosophy. She was also imbued with the thought of St. John
of the Cross. Her major study, *The Science of the Cross*, describes John's theology of the cross for a Europe devastated by the horrors of World War II and
the massive genocide of the Nazi regime.[21] In 1942 she was arrested by the
Gestapo. She and her sister Rosa were taken to Auschwitz where they were
put to death because they were Jewish. Survivors of the atrocities testified
that she had great courage and compassion in dealing with other victims in
the camp.

Simone Weil (1909–1943)

Simone Weil was a French Jewish writer who was deeply drawn to the
Catholic Church although she never converted. She had such high standards
for being a Christian that she felt unworthy on the one hand, but on the other
hand found it impossible to join a church full of so many blemishes. However, many who know her writings consider here a Christian since her intense
devotion to the suffering Christ became central to her writings on affliction.
She explains in her works how every aspect of human experience can be cre-
atively used as channels leading to a further experience of God's presence.
She makes clear that God's disclosure to an individual is always totally gra-
tuitous. Among her writings are *Waiting For God, The Need for Roots, Gravity and Grace*, and *First and Last Notebooks*.[22]

Pierre Teilhard de Chardin (1881–1955)

Teilhard de Chardin was born into an aristocratic French family. As a child he experienced a sense of oneness with nature. Educated by the Jesuits, he joined the Jesuit Order and was ordained a priest in 1911. He did graduate studies in geology and paleontology. In the course of time he had mystical experiences which were stimulated by the vast open spaces of the sea and the desert. He served as a stretcher bearer in the French army during World War I. As a scientist and a mystic he helped impart an optimistic mood to contemporary spirituality. Overall he presented a vision which he expressed in both scientific and poetic language of an evolving universe moving toward a personalized center of consciousness which he called the "omega point" and identified with the cosmic Christ of the late Pauline tradition, notably Paul's Letters to the Colossians and Ephesians. He described this vision of the universe in *Phenomenon of Man* which was published after his death in 1955.[23] Because his works seemed unorthodox and even dangerous to Church officials, he was not allowed to publish anything during his lifetime except his scientific works. In retrospect, the Vatican has expressed some approval of his writings.

In his classic work, *The Divine Milieu*, he describes the presence of God in all creation, the essential goodness of the material world, the intrinsic value of all human activity, and the power of love to unify and personalize our world.[24] These themes helped many Catholics move beyond an otherworldly spirituality that denigrates material reality, human sexuality and personal activity in the world.

Although Chardin's influence has lessened, many elements of his spirituality, which are firmly rooted in a positive understanding of creation and the incarnation, still play an important role in contemporary spirituality.

Thomas Merton (1915–1968)

The best known modern Catholic mystic is probably Thomas Merton who is a powerful witness to the continuing vitality of Christian spirituality in the modern world. His mother was an American and his father was from New Zealand. Merton was born in France and received his early education there and then studied at Cambridge in England. While a student he lived a rather dissolute life and eventually fathered a child. It is rumored that the mother and child died during the Nazi blitz. He continued his studies at Columbia University in New York and after reading Etienne Gilson's *The Spirit of Modern Philosophy* he converted to Catholicism.[25] He then sought entrance into the Franciscan order, but was rejected. Later he was accepted in a monastery of Cistercian Monks of the Strict Observance, better known as Trappists. The monastery he joined is the Abbey of Our Lady of Gethsemani in Kentucky.

Merton's original popularity was based on his best-selling spiritual autobiography, *The Seven Story Mountain* (an image taken from Dante's *Purgatorio*), published in 1946.[26] The book describes his conversion to Catholicism and his early years as a Trappist monk. However, his enduring influence is rooted in his subsequent writing found in his books, letters, poems and articles, all of which reflect the struggles of his spiritual journey. As James C. Bacik writes in *The New Dictionary of Catholic Spirituality*:

> The questions and tensions that haunted Merton's mind and heart are the abiding concerns of contemporary spirituality: how to relate and balance the life of prayer and action; how to reconcile care for nature and the use of modern technology; how to foster personal relationships that lead to God; how to balance the desire for freedom with the demands of authority; how to enter into fruitful dialogue with other religious traditions; and finally how to relate contemplation and the quest for justice.[27]

Bacik correctly points out that Merton represents another feature of contemporary spirituality, namely, the autobiographical style. The personal accounts of his spiritual journey are easy to relate to. This personal narrative style is used by other Catholic spiritual writers such as John Shea and Henri Nouwen. This approach illumines the spiritual life of those who read Merton's works and encourages them to examine their own spiritual life.

Merton entered into meaningful dialogue with members of other Christian denominations and other world religions in order to deepen his understanding of God. He was especially interested in the mystical elements in these religions. Included in his efforts were Orthodox Christians, Protestants, Jews, and Muslims as well as Chinese humanists and Zen Buddhists. The tradition of interfaith spirituality is also found in other Catholic authors such as Raimundo Panikhar, William Johnston and Anthony De Mello. These writers have influenced contemporary spirituality by making insights from Eastern religions available to the Catholic world.

Another aspect of Merton's writing is his effort to combine the mystical and prophetic aspects of the Gospel into a spirituality that incorporates works of justice in a deep inner life. His book *Conjectures of a Guilty Bystander* deals with important social issues of his day.[28] March 18, 1958, Merton experienced his famous Louisville vision which he relates in *Conjectures*. In describing this vision he writes:

> Yesterday, in Louisville, at the corner of 4th and Walnut, suddenly I realized that I love all the people and that none of them were, or could be, totally alien to me.

As if waking from a dream, the dream of my separateness, of my "special" vocation to be different. My vocation does not really make me different from the rest of men or just one in a special category, except artificially, juridically. I am still a member of the human race and what more glorious destiny is there for man, since the Word was made flesh and became, too, a member of the human race.[29]

This statement is quite different from the Merton who entered the Trappists in December 10, 1941, who at the time had a contempt of the world. His embrace now is of the "human race." The Louisville vision clearly shows that he is moving away from the harsh asceticism of his early years as a monk toward becoming the radical humanist of the last decade of his life.[30] The dogmatic, moralistic, world denying man of *The Seven Story Mountain* is the antithesis of the Merton who emerges as the world-embracing monk of the sixties. His newfound, broad inclusiveness finds its expression in numerous essays dealing with racism, arms control, the Cold War, non-violence, and other issues pertaining to social justice. Merton writes:

To choose the world is to choose to do the work I am capable of doing, in collaboration with my brothers, to make the world better, more free, more just, more livable, more human.[31]

For Merton, action and contemplation are not opposed to each other, but are two aspects of the same love of God. As a result, he dealt with many, if not most, of the concerns of contemporary spirituality in his writings. The growing literature on Thomas Merton resulted in many groups devoted to the study of his thought and spiritual practices. His continuing appeal enhances his role as one of the major figures of contemporary spirituality. Merton is an example of the continuing effort to combine the mystical and prophetic aspects of the Christian tradition in a viable spirituality that roots the works of justice in a deep spiritual life.

Dorothy Day (1897–1980)

Dorothy Day continues to influence contemporary spirituality. She was born in Brooklyn, moved to California at six, and to Chicago when she was nine. After high school she attended the University of Illinois for two years. While there she wrote for several campus publications. In 1916 she dropped out of school and moved to New York where she worked as a reporter for a socialist journal and was active in the women's suffrage movement. She married and was divorced and then entered a common-law marriage and gave birth to a daughter, Tamara. She had Tamara baptized and later Dorothy converted to

Catholicism. This brought about a dissolution of her relationship with her husband who did not believe in God and she also became estranged from her radical socialist and Marxist friends.

In 1932 Day met Peter Maurin, a Frenchman who was a strong exponent of the Church's social teachings. He firmly believed that the Gospel calls for concrete action on behalf of the poor. Early in 1933 the two founded the Catholic Worker movement which espoused a radical type of social ethic based on the Gospel. On May 1, 1933, Day published the first edition of *The Catholic Worker*, a monthly paper which she edited for the rest of her life. The circulation of the paper eventually reached over 100,000 and still sells for a penny a copy. The paper strongly opposes the present economic order with its emphasis on profit, wealth and materialism and insists on a personalism stressing the basic equality of all.

Throughout the years, Day took strong positions on a variety of social issues. She supported the right of workers to unionize, child labor laws, and the civil rights movement. She opposed all forms of prejudice, especially anti-Semitism. In the Second World War she held a pacifist position and later opposed the Vietnam War.

The Catholic Worker program established houses of hospitality where the poor and the derelict were fed, clothed and sheltered. The first house of hospitality was opened in the Bowery in New York City in 1933. Many other such houses were opened throughout the United States by members of the movement. There are more than twenty of these houses in the United States today.

From Peter Maurin, Day learned that living out the Gospel is best served within community life. In such an atmosphere individuals support one another and can develop a deep interior life that sustains their service of others. Day insisted on communal spirituality though she found it very difficult at times. She felt this way of life provided an important corrective to the individualism dominant in our culture.

Dorothy Day exemplifies a visible lay spirituality that combines loyalty to the church and respect for its leaders with fidelity to one's personal charism and the courage to take the initiative on behalf of the Gospel. Regular prayer, periodic retreats, and serious study enabled her to respond intelligently to given situations. Her primary ministry was concentrated on the world and its suffering people rather than on the church and its internal life. She set the style and tone for a movement which continues to this day. Her radical spirituality, which is explicitly countercultural, is carried on not only by the Catholic Worker Movement, but also by other peace and justice groups devoted to non-violent approaches which are attempting to help humanize the social, economic, and political spheres.

Dorothy Day died on November 19, 1980. She was buried in a grave provided by the Archdiocese of New York. Her biographer recalls an incident at her funeral that, in many ways, is symbolic of her life. He writes:

> At the church door, Cardinal Terrence Cooke met the body to bless it. As the procession stopped for this rite, a demented person pushed his way through the crowd and bending low over the coffin peered at it intently. No one interfered, because, as even the funeral director understood, it was in such a man that Dorothy had seen the face of God.[32]

Gustavo Gutierrez

Gustavo Gutierrez was born in Lima, Peru, in 1928. He is a Mestizo, part Hispanic and part Quechuan Indian. His family was poor and during his teen years he suffered terribly from osteomyelitis. In his seminary years he studied philosophy and theology. Because of his intellectual gifts he did further theological study in Europe, in Belgium, France and Rome. During this time he was exposed to the writings of progressive European theologians, namely Yves Congar, Karl Rahner, Maurice Blondel and Gerhard von Rad. Upon returning to Lima as a diocesan priest and teacher he attempted to examine the meaning of human existence in the world in which his students lived. He writes:

> This led me to confront Christian faith with thinkers like Albert Camus, Karl Marx, and others as well as film directors like Luis Bunuel and Ingmar Bergman and writers like José María Arguedas.[33]

Later, due to the social and economic conditions in Peru and elsewhere in South America, he became the leading spokesman of liberation theology.

Most observers consider Gutierrez to be the preeminent Latin American liberation theologian. His *Teología de la Liberación,* published in 1971 (the English translation, *A Theology of Liberation,* was published in 1973) is still seen as the cornerstone of liberation theology.[34] Gutierrez and the other liberation theologians believe that the primary task of theology is not to convince the nonbelievers of the "truths" of the Christian faith, but rather it is to help free the oppressed from their inhuman living conditions. In this way the "truth" of theology becomes the "liberation" of the oppressed. Gutierrez uses the term *liberation* in three senses. First, *liberation* refers to freedom from oppressive economic, social, and political systems. Second, *liberation* means that human beings should take control of their own destiny. Third, *liberation* means being emancipated from sin and accepting a new life in Christ. Liberation includes all three meanings and not only the first meaning as some critics indicate. Nevertheless, liberation theology primarily develops the social dimension of faith. Still, it must be emphasized that the basis and point of departure of the theology of liberation is the theological virtue of faith. In fact, it is in virtue of the transcendent dimension of faith that a liberation theology is possible at all.[35]

Gutierrez insists that theology and spirituality must not be estranged from one another. He contends that without a spiritual dimension the struggle against injustice and oppression is in danger of lapsing into bitterness, resentment, and revenge.[36] The richness of classic Christian spirituality is preserved in Gutierrez's writing. For him, the following of Jesus is at the heart of Christian spirituality, wherein meditation on the Scriptures and prayer play a central role.[37] As Alexander Nava writes: "For Gutierrez . . . spiritual theology has its origins in the scriptural mandate to imitate the life of Christ."[38]

Gutierrez believes that spirituality has a corporate as well as an individual modality. The corporate aspect of spirituality, for Gutierrez, is located within particular historical and religious communities. He insists on the accessibility of mysticism to whole groups of marginalized, uneducated, and poor peoples. He argues that liberation theology challenges the monopoly of spirituality by the educated and clerical.

Henri Nouwen

Henri Nouwen was born on January 24, 1932, in the city of Nÿkerk in Holland. He entered the seminary at eighteen and was ordained a priest in 1957. From 1964 to 1966 he studied at the Menninger Institute in Topeka, Kanasa, the birthplace of pastoral psychology and of the development of programs for clinical pastoral education (CPE). At present most of the theological programs in the United States and Western Europe have integrated this discipline into their curricula. At Menninger, Nouwen became friends with John Santos, a Catholic psychologist, who had been invited by Father Theodore Hesburgh to establish a department of psychology at the University of Notre Dame. At Santos' invitation Nouwen became a teacher at Notre Dame from January 1966 to 1968. During the next few years he taught in the Netherlands, first at Amsterdam Joint Pastoral Institute and then at the Catholic Theological Institute of Utrecht.

In 1971 Nouwen returned to the United States to teach at Yale University where he remained until 1981. By now he had written several important books on spirituality and while at Yale he continued his prodigious output including *Reaching Out*, which may well be his most important book during that period.[39] During his tenure at Yale Nouwen lived in a number of interesting places while on sabbaticals. He spent several months living in a Trappist monastery in Piffard, New York, and five months as a scholar in residence in Rome at the North American College. In July 1981, he left Yale. He was 49 years old and his years at Yale had been very fruitful.

From October 1981 through March 1982 he lived in Latin America beginning with a three-month course in Spanish which he took in Cochabamba, Bolivia. Next he spent three months in Lima, Peru, living in a small house in a poor barrio. While in Lima Nouwen met regularly with Gustavo Gutierrez and learned a great deal about liberation theology. As a result his spirituality began to take on more socially critical features, something that had not been very pronounced until then. Upon returning to the United States Nouwen was offered a position at Harvard University. He agreed to teach there for half the year and during the rest of the year he was free to do as he wished. He taught at Harvard for less than three years, from January 1983 until the summer of 1985.

In the Fall of 1983 Nouwen made his first visit to Trosly, a village just north of Paris, France. This was the first community of the L'Arche movement which is dedicated to the care of mentally handicapped people. From August 1985 to August 1986 Nouwen lived and worked with the L'Arche community in Trosly. But from October 1 to 10, 1985, he visited the L'Arche community, "Daybreak," in Richmond Hill, a suburb of Toronto, Canada, and was drawn to that community. At their invitation he became pastor of the "Daybreak" community in August, 1985 where he remained until his death on September 21, 1996.

Nouwen wrote thirty-nine books and it should be noted that most of his journal and magazine articles (revised or not) reappeared in one of his books. His collected works are published by *Continuum* in New York. And as Jurjen Beumer writes in his insightful study of Nouwen:

> The whole broad terrain of mysticism and spirituality, of psychology and pastoral psychology came under his review. What is surprising, however, is that no dry theological textbook appeared out of all this (he never chose to write such a book); instead, all of his reading passed through the filter of his own experience. Theology, faith and church are all very nice and you can say a lot about them, but what kind of impact do they have on you, how do they affect you? This personal approach is what made Nouwen such a beloved and widely read author.[40]

Nouwen has many helpful insights about prayer. He gives an excellent explanation of St. Paul's admonition to "Pray at all time, pray without ceasing, thankful for all, because that is the will of God in Christ Jesus for you." (1 Thess. 5:16–18). In the chapter "Prayer and Thought" which is contained in *Clowning in Rome: Reflections on Solitude, Celibacy, Prayer and Contemplation* he points out that unceasing prayer is not like continuously thinking about God. It is something else. He gives more or less a definition of prayer: "To pray,

I think, does not mean to think about God in contrast to thinking about other things, or to spend time with God instead of spending time with other people. Rather it means to think and live in the presence of God."[41] Every moment must find its origin in prayer. This means one must go through a process of "converting . . . from a self-centered monologue to a God-centered dialogue. In this way we can "lead all our thoughts out of their fearful isolation into a fearless conversation with God."[42]

But the question naturally arises as to how one can begin this loving conversation with God. Nouwen says this can happen by means of good discipline. Discipline means that something very specific and concrete needs to be done to create the context in which a life of uninterrupted prayer can develop. Nouwen writes: "Contemplative prayer can be described as an imagining of Christ, letting him enter fully into our consciousness so that he becomes the icon always present in our inner room."[43] He suggests, for example, that every night before going to sleep one might meditate on the Scripture reading for the next day's Mass. He maintains that in doing so the text remains with us through the night and stays with us. From such a practice a certain familiarity and continuity with God begins to grow.

His approach to reading and meditating on Scripture is clearly summarized in *Reaching Out.* He writes:

> To take the holy scriptures and read them is the first thing we have to do to open ourselves to God's call. Reading the scriptures is not as easy as it seems since in our academic world we tend to make anything and everything we read subject to analysis and discussion. But the word of God should lead us first of all to contemplation and meditation. Instead of taking the words apart, we should bring them together in our innermost being; instead of wondering if we agree or disagree, we should wonder which words are directly spoken to us and connect directly with our most personal story. Instead of thinking about the words as potential subjects for an interesting dialogue or paper, we should be willing to let them penetrate into the most hidden corners of our heart, even to these places where no other word has yet found entrance. Then and only then can the word bear fruit as seed sown in rich soil.[44]

Nouwen did not want to skirt the question of biblical scholarship, but such a scholarly approach was not his first priority. For him, the purpose of spiritual reading is not to master knowledge or information, but to let God's spirit master us. He also believes that reading scripture and silence in God's presence belong together. He writes:

> The word of God draws into silence; silence makes us attentive to God's word. The word of God penetrates through the thick of human verbosity to the silent center of our heart; silence opens in us the space where the word can be heard.

Without reading the word, silence becomes stale, and without silence, the word loses its recreative power.[45]

As for priests and ministers, Nouwen believed theology was very important. But even more important is the need for the future of Christian leadership to present the teachings of the church from a heart that knows God intimately. Presenting theology in an abstract or legalistic manner hinders a spiritual experience of faith. If the spiritual leaders of the church (pastors, bishops, religious, and others) cannot break loose from this approach they prevent the development of a vitally spiritual community. In *Creative Ministry*, he writes:

> It is painful to realize that very few ministers are able to offer the rich mystical tradition of Christianity as a source of rebirth for the generation searching for new life in the midst of the debris of a faltering civilization.[46]

He goes on to say that this is especially needed today since "we are approaching a period of an increased search for spirituality that is the experience of God in the very moment of our existence."[47]

Nouwen has many remarkable insights into the development of Christian spirituality. His books are truly worth reading and heeding. A quotation from *Life of the Beloved: Spiritual Living in a Secular World* is worth noting. It pertains to the fear of death.

> Am I afraid to die? I am every time I let myself be seduced by the noisy voices of my world telling me that my "little self" is all I have and advising me to cling to it with all my might. But when I let these voices move to the background of my life and listen to that small soft voice calling me the Beloved, I know that there is nothing to fear and that dying is the greatest act of love, the act that leads me into the eternal embrace of my God whose love is everlasting.[48]

Nouwen's *Life of the Beloved* together with Cardinal Joseph Bernardin's *The Gift of Peace: Personal Reflections*, are marvelous witnesses to the manner in which a Christian can face death in a loving and noble way.[49]

There are certainly many spiritual writers in the Catholic tradition. Only a select few have been mentioned in this brief overview. All of them can be helpful but by selecting one or two of them as spiritual mentors a person's spiritual development can be greatly fostered.

Chapter Four

Lay Spirituality and Prayer

Lay spirituality in the United States today far exceeds that of any other period in the history of the church in its scope, due in great measure to the large number of educated Catholics. Many Catholics have an appreciation of the living presence of the past and of the continuity of the Christian life and prayer through the centuries. This understanding presupposes a commitment to learning about the richness of their Christian heritage with an understanding that Christians of the past, women and men alike, have bequeathed a great deal of wisdom regarding the life of prayer.

The priesthood of all Christians and their common call to holiness has been summoned back to life by the Second Vatican Council. The Council was an important and institutional turning point, the beginning of a recovery of that earlier vision of the spirituality of the church which stressed the universal call to holiness. *The Dogmatic Constitution on the Church* maintains that all Christians "of whatever rank or status are called to the fullness of Christian life and to the perfection of charity."[1] The same document adopts as its chief theological category the concept of the Church as the entire People of God. Spirituality today is clearly understood as a grassroots phenomenon which pertains to the presence and action of God in the lives of ordinary people who hear the Gospel and respond in the ordinary circumstances of their lives. It is a spirituality of one's everyday life and is frequently expressed in the ordinary circumstances of a person's life. As Edward C. Sellner writes:

> It is a spirituality of the family and the workplace and is frequently expressed in the life of the local parish communities. Since there are many circumstances and types of lay people, there are a great variety of lay spiritualities related to personal vocations, choices, commitments, and lifestyles.

Sellner goes on the say:

Contrary to theological views that arose glorifying the heroic lifestyle of those who chose to be ordained or to live in monastic communities, lay people too have been intimately acquainted with deprivation and human suffering. Their spirituality necessarily has an ascetic dimension to it, for theirs is a daily struggle and discipline to care for their families, maintain careers and jobs, sustain elderly parents and grandparents, contribute volunteer services, find meaning, persist, let go.[2]

To develop one's spirituality it is necessary to maintain a life of prayer. The traditional definition of prayer is the raising of the mind and heart to God. It is the way one enters into conscious, loving communion with God. In fact, prayer is a response to God's initiation of dialogue with us. It is an act whereby we accept ourselves as radically open to the presence of God. When we explicitly are aware of our relationship to God, we are praying. Every action we perform as a way of expressing that relationship is a prayer. Every time we sacrifice our own personal interest for a spiritual purpose we are praying.

The example and teaching of Jesus regarding prayer is the model for Christian prayer. At the beginning of his public ministry when he was baptized by John, "Jesus . . . was praying (Luke 3:21–23). Then he was led by the spirit into the desert where he stayed 40 days fasting and praying to prepare himself for his public ministry (Luke 4:1–13). When his preaching and healing drew large crowds, to fortify himself Jesus "withdrew to deserted places to pray" (Luke 5:16). The Gospel of Mark describes an occasion that illustrates Jesus' habitual practice of prayer. After Jesus had preached in the synagogue at Capernaum and healed Simon's mother-in-law and many other sick people, and had cast out demons, Jesus "rising very early before dawn, left and went off to a deserted place, where he prayed" (Mark 1:35). At important moments in his public life Jesus devoted special time to prayer. For example, before choosing the Twelve, "he departed to the mountain to pray, and he spent the night in prayer to God" (Luke 6:12).

After feeding the multitudes in the desert Jesus again spent the night in prayer (Mark 6:46; Mt. 14:22–23; John 6:15). When his disciples returned from a successful missionary journey Jesus prayed a prayer of gratitude and praise in saying: "I give praise to you, Father, Lord of heaven and earth, for although you have hidden these things from the wise and the learned you have revealed them to the childlike. Yes, Father, such has been your gracious will." (Mt. 11:25–26; Luke 10:21). In addressing God as "Father" or "Abba," Jesus manifested his extraordinary intimacy and union with God as well as his submission to the Father as an obedient son. In Luke's Gospel, it was after observing Jesus at prayer that one of his disciples asked him to teach them to pray. In response Jesus taught them the Lord's Prayer (the Our Father) (Luke 11:1–4). All the references to Jesus at prayer are too numerous to cite here.

What should be noted are the prayers of Jesus at the end of his life. In the Garden of Gethsemani Jesus begged his Father to remove the cup of suffering (the Cross) but his prayer was completed when he prayed that not his will but his Father's will be done (Luke 22:42). On the Cross he prayed for his persecutors (Luke 23:34). He also used the opening verse of Psalm 22 when he cried out: "My God, my God, why have you forsaken me?" (Mark 15:34; Mt. 27:46). Just prior to his death he surrendered himself in prayer to his Father: "Father, into your hands I commend my spirit" (Luke 23:46).

Jesus taught prayer not only by his example, but also by his words of instruction. He tells us, for example: "When you pray, go to your inner room, close the door, and pray to your Father in secret. And your Father who sees in secret will repay you" (Mt 6:6). We are also told that the Father is more concerned about us and is better than any earthly father (Mt. 7:11; Luke 11:11–13). He forgives us as we forgive others (Mark 11:25). We are to pray to avoid succumbing to temptation (Luke 22:46), since the spirit is willing but the flesh is weak (Mk 14:38). We may pray for any good thing we may need (Mt. 7:11). We should pray that laborers be sent into the harvest (Luke 10:2). And we should pray for the gift of the Holy Spirit (Luke 11:13). Jesus also singles out our enemies and persecutors as those for whom we should pray (Mt. 5:44).

The basic advice on how to pray effectively is to pray with faith (Mark 11:22–24). And we are to pray with perseverance, not giving up though we seem not to be heard (Luke 18:1). Most importantly, we are to pray after we are reconciled to our brothers and sisters (Mark 11:25). We are also told that it is important to pray with others: "For where two or three are gathered together in my name, there am I in the midst of them" (Mt. 18:20). Though Jesus gives other instructions the Lord's Prayer expresses the essence of the covenant with his disciples. With the opening phrase, "Our Father who art in heaven," we are told that God is our Father, and therefore we as Christians are brothers and sisters. The first three petitions indicate our duties. We are to praise God, to work for his kingdom, and to do his will. To help us carry out these duties the final four petitions ask for God's help. We ask God to feed us, forgive us, help us to ward off temptation, and preserve us from evil. There is a condition attached to the gift of forgiveness: we must forgive others (Mt. 6:9–15).

There are various *purposes* for prayer. There is the prayer of *adoration*, whose immediate end is the praise and glory of God; the prayer of *thanks-*

giving gives gratitude to God for blessings received; the prayer of *contrition* expresses sorrow for sin; and the prayer of *petition* asks for God's mercy upon oneself or others. In regard to the latter, the prayer of petition is always answered in that it draws us closer to God as do the other forms of prayer. The prayer of petition expresses and deepens our relationship of trust and dependence on God. It also deepens our relationship with those for whom we pray. And, as St. Paul writes: "Have no anxiety at all but in everything, by prayer and petition, with thanksgiving, make your requests known to God" (Phil. 4:6). And those requests can be made for anything we consider to be good for us or others. Prayers are always answered in that one's relationship to God is deepened. However, we can never fully understand the effect of prayer on God, on human history, or on ourselves. The effect of prayer is enshrouded in the mystery of the divine—human relationship. The well-known statement which comes into play here is: "Work as if everything depends on you; but pray as if everything depends on God."

Catholicism offers a variety of important approaches to prayer. Among these are the Eucharist and the other sacraments of the Church. The practice of contemplation and the use of centering prayer are also important for one's spiritual development as will be seen in what follows.

THE EUCHARIST

The Eucharist (Mass) is a liturgical event, a sacramental meal, in which the Church remembers, celebrates, and proclaims Jesus' sacrificial life, death and resurrection. The Second Vatican Council proclaimed that the Eucharist is the "source of the Church's life and the pledge of future glory."[3] The Council also teaches: 1) "No Christian community can be built up unless it has its basis and center in the celebration of the most Holy Eucharist"[4]; 2) It is the "summit" and the "fountain" of the whole Christian life"[5]; and 3) "Day by day the liturgy builds up those within the Church into the Lord's holy temple, into a spiritual dwelling for God—an enterprise which will continue until Christ's full stature is achieved."[6]

During the Eucharist the congregation offers all glory and honor to God. It is a sacramental meal in which the elements of bread and wine become the body and blood of Christ which are shared in faith by those in attendance. The Eucharist is a memorial of Jesus' entire life as evidenced in the reading of Scripture, but most especially it is a memorial of the culmination of his life in his suffering, death and resurrection. It is also a celebration, a solemn act of praise and *thanksgiving* (Eucharist), for what Christ has done for us. In the New Testament the term for the Eucharist is the "breaking of bread" as used in the Gospel of Luke (24:35) and in the Acts of the Apostles (2:42). This term emphasizes that the Eucharist must be shared, that is, those who break bread are expected to share their love with others as Christ did.

In the 16th century the Council of Trent, in response to the Protestant Reformation, put great emphasis on the reality of Christ's presence in the Eucharist and further stated Christ remains present as long as the Eucharistic bread continues to exist. Trent also stressed the objective value of the Eucharistic sacrifice, which makes present in an unbloody manner the sacrifice of Christ which was offered in a bloody manner.

Eucharistic devotion existed prior to the Council of Trent and Eugene La Verdiere points out that the reservation of the Eucharist outside of Mass can be traced at least to St. Justin in the 2nd century.[7] However, it was not until the 13th century that Eucharistic devotions arose. These consisted in private visits to the Blessed Sacrament. Later in the same century public processions with the Blessed Sacrament originated in France in connection with the feast of Corpus Christi and the practice quickly spread throughout Europe. Benediction of the Blessed Sacrament had its origin in the 14th century as a conclusion to evening prayers in monasteries. In all these devotions the primary attitude of those in attendance was adoration. Over time these Eucharistic devotions acquired such importance as to displace the Mass in popular religiosity, at least for some Catholics. Vatican II implemented decrees calling for the simplification but not the elimination, of such Eucharistic devotions. What is central is the Eucharistic celebration during Mass. More will be said concerning devotions in a later chapter.

THE SACRAMENTS

Roman Catholicism believes that the seven sacraments of the Church are key moments in a believer's relationship with Christ. They help one to respond to Christ in a unique manner as well as to be nourished and nurtured by him from the beginning of one's Christian existence to the moment of death. Included in our reflections will be a brief consideration of the history of the sacraments and of the reasons why Catholicism believes there are seven sacraments rather than only two (baptism and the Lord's Supper), which is the teaching of most of Protestant Christianity. Recent changes in the administration of the sacraments, especially those pertaining to the Eucharist (Mass), will also be briefly treated.

In the ancient Roman world, the Latin word *sacramentum* referred to the oath of allegiance taken by a soldier when he was inducted into one of the legions of the Roman army. In the early third century the Christian writer Tertullian referred to baptism as a sacrament in order to emphasize the commitment one made to Jesus when one was baptized. By means of the sacraments, a Christian is helped to "put on a new man" that is, take up a new life-style dedicated to Christ.

The Vulgate (Latin) edition of the Bible uses *sacramentum* to translate the Greek word *mysterion* (mystery), a term used by St. Paul in reference to the "hidden plan" by which God intended to save, renew, and unite all things in Christ (Eph. 1:9 and 3:3–9). Early Christian authors, writing in Greek, often spoke of Christian "mysteries" in relationship to many of the rituals and prayers that were being used by the Church. A special place was given among these mysteries to a series of actions leading to one's final initiation as a Christian. Among these actions were found Lenten instructions, anointing, profession of faith, and finally baptism itself. St. Augustine, who died in A.D. 430 and was the most influential Christian writer of the first millennium, said a sacrament is a holy sign (symbol) through which a Christian perceived and received Christ's grace. He said this sign is made up of two essential parts, a material component (e.g., water in baptism) and the spoken word of conferral (e.g., "I baptize you in the name of the Father, and of the Son, and of the Holy Spirit"). Despite such definitions, Christian writers continued to refer to a variety of other rites as sacraments, including the sign of the cross, the anointing of kings, the reception of ashes on Ash Wednesday, and the Trinity (e.g., in the mid-twelfth century St. Bernard of Clairvaux referred to the Trinity as the mysterious oneness of the three divine persons and as a great sacrament to be worshiped rather than investigated).

Peter Lombard, who died in A.D. 1159, in his famous *Book of Sentences,* which was a standard textbook for Christian theologians until well into the seventeenth century, argued that there were only seven sacraments. St. Thomas Aquinas and most Catholic writers essentially agreed with Lombard's reasoning. In the sixteenth century, Protestant reformers such as Martin Luther and John Calvin argued that, according to the strict word of Scripture, only two sacraments were instituted and ordained by Christ as signs and means of grace: baptism and the Lord's Supper. The Catholic response to the Protestant reformers came at the Council of Trent, which formally defined the seven sacraments: baptism, Eucharist (the Lord's Supper), confirmation, reconciliation (confession), marriage, holy orders, and the anointing of the sick. All were instituted by Christ as sacraments, even though the biblical testimony is not equally clear for all seven. Above all, the Council of Trent's response to the Protestant reformers was a strong statement of support for the sacraments, which contrasted sharply with the eventual Protestant tendency to subordinate the sacraments to the preached sermon.[8]

Modern Catholic theologians such as Edward Schillebeeckx and the late Karl Rahner have applied the term *sacrament* in a wider sense than simply to the seven sacraments.[9] Christ himself, as the Word of God become human, is understood as the primordial sacrament of one's encounter with God. God's love for the human race becomes visible in Jesus as a great sign, as does God's saving mercy in Jesus's death on the Cross, and his resurrection from the dead.

In addition, the Christian church (which includes all Christians) is understood as the basic sacrament of Jesus. The Church is both sign and cause (as instrument) of the ultimate unity of all things in Christ. And, as is so well pointed out in *An American Catholic Catechism*, the wider use of the term *sacrament* is an indication that the sacraments of the Church are being understood less as detached events of grace between God and humankind than as meaningful moments within God's plan of salvation.[10] The sacraments are rites of incorporation in which Christ draws men and women more fully under the influence of his redeeming grace and his saving mission. The sacraments are indeed events of grace, integrated into the life of Christians, in which the Spirit of God is imparted by the Lord who is ever sending his Spirit into the world. In the sacraments, incorporation and grace are extended through symbolic or ritual actions of human communication and worship in the Church in the form of initiation (baptism), reconciliation (confession), a community meal (Eucharist), or a marriage commitment. In the sacraments, both the community and individuals give expression to their faith and, under the influence of the Holy Spirit, develop and deepen this fundamental receptivity to Christ's presence and influence.

Catholic doctrine teaches that each of the seven sacraments responds to a deep personal need for Christ's redemptive presence at critical moments in each person's life-history. A succinct analysis of the seven sacraments and the role each plays in one's life is given in *An American Catholic Catechism*. The following passage deserves to be quoted in its entirety.

> *Baptism* envelops the beginning of life in God's loving kindness and stamps it with the irrevocable concern of Christ and his assembled people. As a person approaches maturity, *Confirmation* renews the gift of God's spirit as the source of strength and support in a life of discipleship and service. In ecclesiastical *penance*, we can deal with the cancer of sin and the wounds of guilt and infidelity by approaching the Lord, "a God merciful and gracious, slow to anger, . . . forgiving iniquity and transgress of sin" (Ex. 34:6). When serious illness threatens to engulf us in self-concern, *sacramental anointing* brings God's presence and assimilates us to Christ who suffered on behalf of many. *Ordination* and *marriage* are sacramental dedications of mature Christians to the lifelong vocations of loving service to which God calls them.

Our basic problem, however, the one that accompanies us for a lifetime, is the way we relate to other people. Can we overcome the stifling effect of self-seeking so as to live in peace with others? Can we grow in prompt readiness to help and serve the Christ who calls to us through people in need? Thus, God would have us return constantly to the *eucharistic meal* where we and those near to us are made one body in Christ and where we are inserted into Christ's selfless giving of himself on behalf of every human person. Through the sacraments, therefore, the course of our personal lives is repeatedly punctuated by God's loving presence at just the moments of our greatest need of him.[11]

It is clear, then, that in the term *sacrament* there is found the concrete reality of the life of every Christian. Thus the word should not be understood only as referring to seven efficacious rites. It should be taken to mean that the people of God, as an ecclesiastical community, is transformed into a sacrament. In other words, there is a visible community of human beings living in actual contact with the rest of humankind that, through its existential actions, contains, manifests, and communicates the saving presence of Christ. Such sacramentality implies that Christians should adopt an attitude that goes far beyond ritualism or moralism. Instead of concentrating primarily on devotions and religious practices that are simply a means to an end, Christians should dedicate themselves to the work of being true and efficacious signs of salvation, a demanding and vital task.

The renewal of the sacramentality of the Church that began at Vatican II is aimed at helping Catholics to understand the symbolic value of each sacrament in order to help them become better witnesses of Christ. For example, confessions are now heard face-to-face, if one so desires. This format is much more personal than the anonymity of the confessional, and many find it more spiritually beneficial. Stress is also placed on the fact that in the sacrament of reconciliation the priest represents not only Christ but the community of Christ as well, since all sin is not only against God, but violates the love relationship of the community as a whole. The marriage ceremony, always so beautiful, is more so now. Couples have much more input in the service. They may choose the Scriptures, ask family or friends to serve as lectors, and select the music. This greatly adds to the celebration of marriage and manifests in a unique way the couples' personal relationship with Christ as well as the community involvement of their fellow Christians. Among other things, the newly married couple pledge that they will be true signs of Christ. This personalism and sense of community is also found in the baptismal rite, be it that of an infant or an adult. In the baptism of an infant, for example, great stress is placed on the responsibility of the parents and godparents, as well as on the immediate community, to nurture the baby in the ways of Christ. Any sense of magic attached to the ritual, even though mistakenly, has been put to rest.

At Mass, the sense of personalism and community has been greatly strengthened by the inclusion of all as participants, whether it be by all worshipers responding to the prayers of the celebrant, by the community joining in the hymns, by the reception of the Eucharist in one's hands (as a sign of inclusion in the priesthood of the faithful), by the exchange of the kiss of peace, or in various other ways. All of these changes are meant to help Catholics deepen their relationship with Christ.

In regard to the sacraments, perhaps the most dramatic occurrence was the change at Mass from Latin to the vernacular. This was done to help augment the participation of all in attendance and to strengthen the sense of Christian community. It is interesting to note that the first official decree of Vatican II, *The Constitution on the Sacred Liturgy* issued on September 29, 1963, was a broad plan for liturgical reform that was to be implemented during the following months and years. In fact, by 1970 the essential changes had been completed. The changes began in April of 1964 when, at communion, Catholics began answering "Amen" as the priest gave them the host and said, "Corpus Christi" ("The Body of Christ"). As insignificant as it may seem, this "Amen" was the beginning of a greater personal and community involvement. On the first Sunday of Advent that same year, American Catholics went to Mass and heard their first official half-English, half-Latin Mass. This was rather confusing since the congregation read their prayers and responses in English and then watched as the priest shifted back to Latin for the recital of orations, the canon, and all prayers recited only by himself. Laity were chosen to read the Epistle and Responsorial. In November of 1964, Pope Paul VI then reduced the eucharistic fast to one hour, rather than from midnight of the night before, and water was allowed to be taken at any time. These changes in the fasting laws were made to encourage greater numbers of Catholics to more fully participate in the Mass by receiving Holy Communion. The difficulty of the previous fasting laws made it rather burdensome for many to receive communion.

Altars were being turned around in 1964, and for some this resulted in self-consciousness at finding oneself being so directly addressed by the celebrant. It was equally difficult for many priests. The ingrained habits of years had to be broken. The priest had to learn new attitudes toward the rubrics of the Mass again when, in May of 1967, Rome eliminated numerous genuflections, altar kissing, signs of the cross over the offerings, and the custom of keeping thumbs and forefingers joined after the consecration of the bread and wine. During the same month, permission was given for the Latin canon to be read aloud and for the English (vernacular) translation of the canon to be prepared. Saturday evening Masses were officially approved, along with the practice of receiving communion while standing. In the spring of 1969 the new lectionary was completed and a new Order of Mass was published that gave a framework that would not need substantial alternation in the near future. The entire Mass was now in English. Further, the rubrics frequently called attention to the need for flexibility, adaptation, and imagination. Since 1970 Catholics have learned, though at times with great difficulty, that different styles of liturgy are needed for different people, since there are so many subjective differences among the faithful. They have also learned that not all the Sunday Masses need to be celebrated in exactly the same modality. Accepted differences in music and style for the good of the community were established.

Many Catholics were greatly troubled when the Latin Mass was changed. There are several reasons for this kind of reaction. Because the Latin Mass had symbolized the unity of Catholicism (the Mass was said exactly the same everywhere in the world) some felt the changes were the beginning of disunity. They failed to see the difference between unity and uniformity, which was understandable since the Catholic Mass had not changed since the introduction of the Tridentine (from the Council of Trent) Mass in 1570. The Latin Mass, especially when accompanied by Gregorian music, was aesthetically beautiful, far more so than the Mass as presently recited in English. Still, it is difficult to explain the survival of Latin in the liturgy during a four-hundred-year period (1570–1963) that saw the language die while being transformed into the Romance languages of Europe. One reason, undoubtedly, was that the liturgy in the vernacular had been regarded by Catholics since the sixteenth century as the mark of Protestantism. Since there was so much hostility between Catholics and Protestants, it seemed unreasonable to adapt to a liturgical style that would give credibility to what Protestantism had opted for at its very inception. Some also felt that the Latin Mass symbolized the timeless and changeless reality of Roman Catholicism. But this simply was not so. The Roman Catholic Church has never been timeless or changeless. As Vatican II clearly points out, Christians are the pilgrim people of God. Nonetheless, such was the perception of many Catholics, a perception that had been fostered by attitudes conveyed in the *Baltimore Catechism* as well as many other instructional manuals. Ultimately, the liturgical changes inaugurated by the Vatican Council, including the use of the vernacular, were brought about to allow the laity (few of whom knew Latin) to become active participants at the Mass. Such participation was fostered to underscore the idea that Mass, by its very nature, is not a private devotion but a community action. In the judgment of most observers in the Church, the long-term effects of this change will surely strengthen the unity of Roman Catholicism.

For the sacraments to be meaningful they must stem from a vital Christian community, a Christ-centered discipleship. This means that stress must be placed on the local community, the parish. Roman Catholicism is composed of thousands upon thousands of such local parishes, and each parish must constantly strive to represent Christ. We should recall here that just as Jesus is the primary sacramental sign of the Father, so is the Church the primary sacramental sign of Jesus. But the Church does not exist in theory alone. The Church, the People of God, exists primarily in the concrete, in the local Christian community, in the parish.[12] No two parishes will ever be exactly alike since the lives of their parishioners are lived, at least to some extent, under different circumstances. Such differences are manifest when comparing Catholic parishes in different countries such as, for example, the United States and Nicaragua. There are often great differences in the operations of parishes within the same city. The Word of God must come alive in different situations and different contexts. The Gospel must be translated in terms of real-life situations and this process must be celebrated within a given situation, culture, and historical moment. Here we enter the broad domain of liturgy, which includes the seven sacraments, but much more besides. It includes the whole range of Christian life that encompasses social justice, ecumenism, and love of neighbor. If the parish is vibrant, the sense of Christian community will become clearer with each passing day. But in a vitalized Christian parish that is truly a sacramental sign of Christ, its members will continually rediscover and live the mystery of Christ found in the Scriptures and with ever greater appreciation will come to understand how they are encountered by Christ. They will also come to understand more fully how Christ is encountered not only in the sacraments but even in the most prosaic events of the day.

A question that is often raised by other Christians concerns the Catholic belief that there are seven sacraments. Protestant Christianity believes there are only two sacraments, baptism and the Lord's Supper. Both are acknowledged by Jesus and are clearly attested in Scripture: baptism in John 3:5, Mt. 28:18–19, and Mark 16:6, etc.; and the Eucharist in Mt. 26:26–28, Luke 22:14–20, and Mark 14:22–25, etc. But regarding the other five, Protestant Christianity believes their institution by Christ is nowhere to be found in the Bible. Catholicism, on the other hand, officially teaches that there are seven sacraments and that all seven were instituted by Christ. Scriptural references are, in fact, provided by the Bible for the other five. For example, concerning confirmation read Acts 8:15–17; for reconciliation, Mt. 16:19 and John 20:19–23; for marriage, Mt. 19:3–9 and Ephesians 5:13–33; for holy orders, 2 Tim. 1:6; and for the anointing of the sick, Luke 5:13–18 and James 5:14–15.

Nevertheless, Catholicism substantiates the sevenfold nature of the sacraments not by biblical prooftexting. As a matter of fact it allows that the biblical evidence is not necessarily sufficient to justify all seven sacraments. Rather, Catholicism begins with the notion that the Church itself, as the primordial sacrament of Christ, is the visible earthly representation of the grace of redemption. Catholicism also argues that Christ himself laid down the sevenfold direction of the visible sacramental acts of the Church.[13] Scriptural data exist for baptism, reconciliation, the Eucharist, holy orders, and to a certain extent, confirmation. As for matrimony and the sacrament of anointing of the sick, it is more difficult to produce data referring explicitly to Christ's will. But Catholicism does presuppose the implicit will of Christ in regard to these sacraments. Catholics experience the actuality of these sacraments and believe they are de facto acts that are fundamentally expressive of the life of the Church. The Church understands her own nature by experiencing it. The Church recognizes these acts that flow from her sacramental nature as fundamentally and unconditionally the fruits of that nature, and so they are recognized as truly sacramental actions. The Church could not deduce the sevenfold nature of the sacraments in the abstract but instead recognizes its essence in its concrete fulfillment.

As far as the sacraments that are not clearly found in Scripture are concerned, namely confirmation, matrimony, and the anointing of the sick, Catholicism presupposes that the implicit will of Christ is responsible for their existence. In regard to the anointing of the sick, the Church was led in its decision through the apostle's practice of this action in James 5:14–15. Such a conclusion is consistent with the messianic healing of the sick that was quite evidently intended by Christ to be carried out by the early Church. Concerning marriage, St. Paul gives a Christian appreciation of its role in God's plan and sees the conjugal relationship of husband and wife as an image of the relationship between Christ and the Church (Eph. 5:25–33). This bond, in turn, stresses the preexisting connection between the Church (the sacramental sign of salvation) and matrimony as a sacramental sign. Concerning confirmation, Christ did not say to the apostles at a given moment that he was instituting this sacrament. However, during his earthly life he did promise the Holy Spirit to them, and on Pentecost Sunday he sent the Holy Spirit in the form of tongues of fire (Acts 2:3). In order that all Christians might receive the same spirit, the apostles adopted the rite of laying their hands upon the heads of believers as the sign and seal of the gift of the Holy Spirit. In adopting the form of laying on of hands, they were following a gesture often used by Christ himself who laid his hands on people while healing, blessing children, and working miracles.

The sacraments are special moments in the life of a Christian. They can be prepared for and intensified in the everyday acts of life that are performed out of love for Christ. But they can also be weakened by not attempting to live one's day in a loving Christian fashion, but rather by giving in to selfishness and self-serving attitudes. Thus, the sacraments cannot be isolated from the organic unity of a full Christian life. They are culminating moments in one's

Christian journey and should never be considered isolated actions.[14] It is very important to see the sacraments in relationship to the whole of Christian life. This can be done by comparing the Christian life to marriage. For example, when a married couple makes love, which is a sacramental act, it is not automatically fulfilling of that couple's relationship. Rather it is dependent on the manner in which the man and woman have related to each other in those actions preceding the act of intercourse. If they have been considerate, affectionate, and tender to each other in the everyday events preceding intercourse, the act itself will be truly representative of those moments and will indeed be symbolic of their love and, thus, a culminating event. But if they have been inconsiderate, harsh, and lacking in tenderness, the act of intercourse will not be as fulfilling as it should be. This does not negate the act, but it does describe the kind of preparatory qualities needed to allow the act to be as fulfilling as possible. The same preconditions apply to the Eucharist. Surely it is important that one receive communion at Mass, which itself is a table fellowship with Christ. But the sacrament will be a greater or lesser sign of one's relationship with Christ depending on the quality of one's love of Christ and love of neighbor as determined by one's daily actions and on the quality of one's habit of prayer and meditation.

A final statement about the meaning of the sacraments should be made. It can happen that one's experience of God may indeed by more intense outside the sacraments than during the moment one receives them. An encounter with a loved one by means of a letter, a tender smile or touch, the majesty of a sunset, and a variety of other possibilities—all these may bring one to feel God's presence with greater intensity than may ever occur in the reception of a sacrament. Such bestowals of grace may, in fact, raise a Christian to greater spiritual heights than the sacraments themselves. It should be understood that the sacraments determine the objective importance of certain moments in life. However, besides such moments that are objectively decisive, there surely can be others that subjectively are of vital importance. For those who love Christ their relationship to him is constant, and there are many moments in such a relationship that are not produced by the sacraments per se. Rather, the sacraments are necessary as important markers, as milestones along the way, so that by living the Christian life to its fullest an individual may become more and more one with Christ.

CONTEMPLATION

Contemplation is a way of making oneself aware of the presence of God who is always present. Awareness is central to contemplation and is different from meditation which involves discursive reason. Reasoning involves a subject thinking and an object thought about. Contemplation is a very different experience from thinking in that the awareness of the presence of God is apprehended not by thought but by love. And it tends always to be unitive. In contemplation one's subjectivity becomes one with the subjectivity of God and the individual contemplating seems to disappear. The self remains distinct from God since it is not God, yet it is inseparable from God.

Contemplation is not a method of prayer to be chosen at will. It is a gift into which one is drawn. Its most intense form is attained when there is ecstatic union between the individual and God so that the human senses can no longer communicate with the outside world at that moment. This is often referred to as rapture.

In discussing prayer there is a useful distinction which was previously noted. "Kataphatic" ("affirmative") prayer uses words and images as when a person meditates. "Apophatic" ("negative") prayer is simply silence in the presence of God, and such prayer is a kind of contemplation.

Thomas Merton in his earlier writings such as *The Seven Story Mountain* spoke of contemplation as though it were restricted to the monastic life.[15] However, he calls people "in the world" to become as much like monks as possible. Many people from various religious backgrounds ignored Merton's elitist attitude and used what he said about monastic contemplation in ways more congenial to their lifestyle. As Merton matured he moved toward the opinion that contemplation is the goal of life for all. Vatican II's teaching that everyone is called to holiness would surely seem to vindicate his view that everyone is called to the contemplative life.

In his writings Merton expresses his strong preference for the apophatic approach. He writes:

> Now, while the Christian contemplative must certainly develop by the study of the theological understanding of concepts about God, he is called mainly to penetrate the worldless darkness and apophatic light of an experience beyond concepts. . . . Relinquishing every attempt to grasp God in limited human concepts, the contemplative's act of submission and faith attains to His presence and His reality as the ground of being itself.[16]

CENTERING PRAYER

Centering prayer is a special method of contemplation in which one simply attends to the presence of God at the center of their person. A mantra such as "Jesus is Lord" is sometimes repeated to keep one's attention centered.

Centering prayer is a method designed to facilitate the development of contemplative prayer by preparing one's mind to accept this gift. It is not meant to replace all other kinds of prayer, but simply puts other kinds of prayer into a new and fuller perspective. Our way of seeing reality changes in this process. As Thomas Keating observes: "A restructuring of consciousness takes place that empowers us to perceive, relate to, and respond with increasing sensitivity to the divine presence and action in, through, and beyond everything that exists."[17]

Keating advises that centering prayer is not an end in itself, but a beginning. It is not done for the sake of enjoying spiritual consolation, but for the sake of its positive results such as charity, peace, joy, self-knowledge, compassion, inner freedom and humility. Keating believes that centering prayer must be done regularly, preferably twice a day for about a half hour each time. Other practices can be carried out during the day such as repetition of a short prayer, unconditional acceptance of others, or letting go of upsetting emotions as soon as they arise.

Thomas Keating is a Cistercian monk and the former abbot of St. Joseph's Abbey in Spencer, Massachusetts. He is the founder of the Centering Prayer movement. He gives retreats on Centering Prayer throughout the year, and he gives the following outline of the Centering Prayer method.

1) Choose a sacred word as the symbol of your intention to open and yield to God's presence and action within. The sacred word could be one of the names of God or a word that you feel comfortable with, e.g. presence, silence, peace, stillness, oneness.
2) Sitting comfortably and with eyes closed, settle briefly and silently introduce the sacred word as the symbol of your consent to God's presence and action within.
3) When you become aware of thoughts, return ever so gently to the sacred word. This is the only activity you initiate once the period of centering prayer has begun.
4) The term *thoughts* includes any perception at all, e.g., sense perceptions, feelings, images, memories, reflections and commentaries. During the prayer time, avoid analyzing your experience, harboring expectations, or aiming at some specific goal, such as having no thoughts, making the mind a blank, feeling peaceful or consoled, repeating the sacred word continuously, or achieving a spiritual experience.
5) At the end of the prayer time, remain in silence with eyes closed for a couple of minutes. This gives the psyche a brief space to readjust to the external senses and a better chance of bringing the atmosphere of interior silence into the activities of daily life.[18]

Keating is an excellent writer and for further insights into his thoughts concerning spirituality and spiritual growth the following books authored by him would surely be helpful: *Open Mind, Open Heart: The Contemplative Dimension of the Gospel*;[19] *The Mystery of Christ: The Liturgy as Spiritual Experience*;[20] and *Reawakenings*.[21]

Chapter Five

Catholic Feminist Theology
and Spirituality

Feminist theology is the critique of the bias which conceptualizes God as male and in which male experience is assumed to be normative for all human experience. It further criticizes the notion which identifies women as carnal and irrational and which maintains that women are responsible for the entrance of sin into the world. Catherine Mowry La Cugna writes:

> The project of theological feminism is to recover women's experience and integrate it into theological reflection, to search the tradition for what has contributed to women's subjugation and to search the tradition also for liberating elements (for example, the ministry of Jesus to outcasts; his self-revelation and post resurrection appearances to women).[1]

One of the most significant developments since Vatican II has been the development of feminist spirituality. As Anne Carr states:

> It is the spirituality of those who have experienced feminist consciousness raising and so have critical questions about inherited patterns and assumptions about gender differences and the implications of these for social and ecclesial roles and behavior.[2]

Carr believes that feminist spirituality is for men as well as women. In fact it is for all those who are deeply aware of the historical and cultural restrictions which have been placed upon women in the church and in society at large. Because of its sense of universal solidarity, feminist spirituality opposes all forms of human oppression, including racism, classism, sexism, and elitism. It is also global in its outlook and opposes militarism and the exploitation of the environment. Feminist authors suggest that God can at least at times be imagined and worshipped as mother and sister, and that Jesus thought of in a nonandrocentric way as having the feminine qualities of the biblical Wisdom as well as the masculine features which he manifested.

Catholic women who have adopted a feminist spirituality have done so for a variety of reasons. As Sandra M. Schneiders writes in *The New Dictionary of Catholic Spirituality* concerning the reasons why many (though not the majority) of Catholic women have become feminists:

> They have seen the implications of their feminism for their spiritual lives. The oppressive masculinity of liturgical language, the maleness of the God image that controls their religious imagination, their domination by men through the sacramental system, the marginality of women in the biblical tradition, the exclusion of female experience and wisdom from the theological and moral tradition of the church, women's subordination in ministry, and the effective sexual apartheid in the institutional church have become more and more obvious, painful, and finally intolerable.[3]

Anne Carr argues that for women who remain committed to Christ and the Church, traditional symbols and noninclusive interpretations of them are not the starting point of feminist spirituality. Rather the starting point is women's "present experience" in the Church—their experience of its communal life, of the sacraments, of the preaching of the Gospel, and of "the corporate and graced awareness of critical Christian feminism."[4] She adds that what women find in the Jesus of the Gospels is a person of remarkable openness to women as evidenced by his inclusion of women among his disciples, his friendship with Mary Magdalene, his positive use of women in his parables, his breaking of taboos in speaking with the Samaritan woman and the Syro-Phoenician women, and the role of women as the first witnesses of the resurrection. Carr writes: "The theological symbols of Christian tradition are interpreted today by women within this narrative context that the New Testament stories provide."[5] She adds that the Church has a pluralism of manifestations and that "the scholarly recovery of the 'lost' history of women in the early Christian communities is significant."[6] She cites Elisabeth Schusaler Fiorenza's work as "especially suggestive about the character of the earliest Christian churches as radically egalitarian, inclusive of marginal people (women and slaves), and counterculture."[7] Fiorenza has produced a number of important books in recent years and the foundation of contemporary feminist Christology is in great measure due to her ground-breaking book, *In Memory of Her: A Feminist Theological Reconstruction of Christian Origins.*[8]

The mission of the church is one of service to people, especially the poor, the oppressed, and the marginalized. Although structures of authority are necessary for this mission, those structures are always subordinate to it and are to be judged by their capacity to enable the church to fulfill the mission.

Feminist theology, as Anne Carr notes, rejects a "patriarchal model of the church in which the focus on authority and obedience is one of coercive power that suggests distrust of the members who are envisioned more as children than as responsible adults."[9] Therefore, Christian feminist women are deeply involved in the transition from a patriarchal to an egalitarian model of the church.

The feminist critique of Catholic theology and worship maintains that the exclusive, literal, and patriarchal use of masculine language and images for God borders on the idolatrous. The critique rests on the axiom that God transcends all words, concepts, and images. Richard P. McBrien points out that in spite of the rich diversity of images and metaphors for God in the Bible, prevailing Christian language names God exclusively in male terms, forgetting or marginalizing the rest. He goes on to say:

> And when these images are used, as in the case of God the *Father*, they are taken literally. As if God had all the properties and characteristics of a human father. Finally, the paradigm for the symbol of God emerges from a world in which men rule within a patriarchal system.[10]

Elizabeth A. Johnson in her book, *She Who Is: The Mystery of God in a Feminist Theological Discourse* proposes three strategies for speaking of God in a manner free from oppressive language. First, because of the long history of the word "God" in Christian theology and worship, the word should be continued to be used, but "pointed in new directions through association with metaphors and values arising from women's experience." Second, because the exclusive use of the word "God" would run the risk of suppressing many of the most prized characteristics of God's relationship to the world, such as fidelity, compassion and liberating love, it is appropriate to speak of God in personal symbols. But to counteract the persistent and corrosive dominance of male symbolism for God, those personal symbols must be reflective of, and emerge from, the actual experience of women. Third, those symbols should not simply ascribe feminine qualities to God or disclose a feminine dimension in God. God-language must express the fullness of female humanity as well as of male humanity and of the world of nature "in equivalent ways."[11]

God certainly transcends sex and gender and is the Creator of both male and female in the divine image. As a result, either term (male/female) can be used to point to the Godhead. For example, in each of the parallel parables of the shepherd looking for his lost sheep and the homemaker looking for her lost coin (Luke 15:4–10), the central figure seeks what is lost and rejoices with others when it is found. Concerning these parables, Richard P. McBrien writes:

Using traditional men's and women's work, both parables direct the hearer to God's redeeming action with the use of images that are equivalently male and female. The woman with the coins is no less an image of God than is the shepherd with the sheep. But the use of such equivalent language invalidates traditional stereotyping wherein the major work of redemption in the world is done by men, while women are excluded or marginalized.[12]

Rosemary Reuther in the final section of her book, *Women Church: Theology and Practice of Feminist Liturgical Communities* presents new versions of traditional sacramental and liturgical forms as well as new forms of ritual that will sacramentalize women's rites of passage that have been ignored or downplayed in the past: the onset of menstruation, the break from parents' home to living on one's own, marriage, divorce, coming out as a lesbian, embarking on new stages of life, menopause, sickness, and death. She also discusses rituals for the healing of raped women, for battered and sexually abused women, for women who have had miscarriages, and so forth. In the past these situations were covered with shame, as if women themselves were at fault. Reuther maintains that "the creation of liturgy is properly a function of local communities who are engaged in a collective project woven from the fabric of many concrete stories that make up the lives of each member of that body."[13]

A serious question which continues to impact feminine spirituality is the role of women in the official ministry of the Church. Often the particular response to this question produces great emotion. Some consider the idea of women serving the Church as deacons or priests to be a ludicrous betrayal of the Bible and of Catholic tradition and see such a notion as just another aspect of the kind of stridency they associate with the women's movement in general. After all, does not Paul say that women must maintain absolute silence in church (1 Tim. 2:9–15), wear head coverings (1 Cor. 11:10), and perform no official functions in the church except to teach younger women? Another and quite different response comes from those who maintain that the time is long past due for Catholic women to be given the same opportunities as men in serving the Church. Women by baptism are members of Christ's "royal priesthood" and we read in Galatians 3:28 that in Christ there is "neither male nor female but all are one in him." Those who respond this way believe that quotations given about silence, head coverings, and the like are simply cultural phenomena and conditioned statements that are not to be applied literally. In order to arrive at a deeper insight into the reasons for the present controversy, we will have to consider the scriptural references already given in relationship to St. Paul's attitude toward women in public ministry, together with what we read in the Gospels concerning Jesus' attitude and his

statements about women. Though space will not allow a complete treatment
of these biblical passages, insights into relevant scriptural statements will be
given that should shed more light on the issues under discussion. The praxis
of the early Church must also be considered as must the official teaching of
today's Vatican.

The questions concerning the rights of Catholic women to participate in
the fullness of church life are certainly a part of the consciousness-raising in
regard to women that is taking place at so many levels throughout society.
This phenomenon began about two hundred years ago as the result of the
eighteenth-century Enlightenment that advocated the natural rights of every
individual, including women. It is also the product of several larger movements since that time including, among others, the Industrial Revolution, the
educational revolution, the suffragist movement, and finally World War I and
World War II. Although the Industrial Revolution produced some very negative results such as inhumane working conditions and acute social disloca-
tion, it spawned many positive breakthroughs as well. For the first time in
Western society jobs were open to women outside the home on a large scale.
Their world had widened. Also in the nineteenth century, the educational revolution made elementary education available to females as well as males,
while higher education was also made available to some women. The suffragist movement gained the general right for women to vote in public elections
in the United States immediately after World War I. Full citizenship raised
their self-esteem and gave women an important tool to promote further reforms. World War I and World War II, which gave women greater opportunities in the job market while many men served in the military, also helped but-
tress women's self-esteem. A natural concomitant of all these changes was the
stimulus to challenge many of the traditional ideas and regulations that the
male-dominated society of the West inherited from the Greco-Roman tradition. And since the Church is a vital part of society, it is not surprising that
important questions are being raised concerning the role of women in the life
of the Church.

As a matter of fact, Vatican II asserted in *The Decree on the Apostolate of
the Laity* that "since in our times women have an ever more active share in
the whole of society, it is very important that they participate more widely
also in the various fields of the Church's apostolate."[14] This attitude was reaf-
firmed at the third Synod of Bishops that met in Rome in 1971: "We also urge
that women should have their own share of responsibility and participation in
the community life of society and likewise of the Church."[15] And yet women
are, in fact and by law, excluded from the official ordained ministry of the
Church. Both Pope Paul VI and now Pope John Paul II and Pope Benedict
XVI have made it very clear that the Church has no intention of changing the

status of women vis-à-vis ordination into the official ministry of the Church. The Popes based their positions on the constant tradition of the Church. The same argument was used by the Sacred Congregation of the Doctrine of the Faith in 1976, which wrote that this constant tradition was rooted in the practice of Jesus and the apostles. It summarized the present position of the hierarchy with the statement that "the Church, in fidelity to the example of the Lord, does not consider herself authorized to admit women to priestly ordination." The text can be found in *Women Priests: A Catholic Commentary on the Vatican Declaration*, edited by Leonard Swidler and Arlene Swidler.[16]

It is clear that the crux of the problem with the ordination of women is rooted in the biblical interpretation of the practice of Jesus and the apostles as found in the New Testament. It is also evident that on the subject of women and ministry, many have read the Scriptures from the point of view of a theological presupposition that women are inferior to men, as based on the teachings of the Church Fathers, including both St. Augustine and St. Thomas Aquinas. The question facing biblical studies today is whether, such negative presuppositions not withstanding, the New Testament church allowed or disallowed women to serve in the ordained ministry of the Church. Even such a profound scripture scholar as Fr. Raymond Brown in his book *Biblical Reflections on Crises Facing the Church* disclaims his ability to determine the answer to this question in any absolute sense.[17] He simply attempts to make a contribution that, though partial, will help those seeking a solution to this problem.

Likewise, we are presenting a synopsis of some of the more important elements of the problem, not a full treatment of the issues. Therefore, we can only hope that what is said will provide readers with salient information and will encourage them to study the Scriptures with a fresher understanding of what the Bible may or may not be saying concerning ordained female ministers. In treating this issue, it will be necessary to ask if Jesus called women to the ministry and whether or not women participated in the ministry of the New Testament church. Finally, it will be important to determine whether or not there is anything inherent in the character of Christian ministry as found in the New Testament that would mandate the inclusion or exclusion of women.

Much of the received tradition regarding women's roles in the Church was established by the writings of the Church Fathers from the second through sixth centuries. These early theologians discussed women in a contemptuous manner, equating them with Eve, who is herself seen as the archetypal seductress. They recognize that women are baptized and redeemed by Christ; yet they seem to question whether women are fully redeemed. They wonder often whether women are not still cursed by God. Indeed, a dark note of doubt and denigration runs through all of patristic literature. Tertullian, a clergyman of the North African church writing early in the third century, summarizes this attitude when discussing the manner in which women should dress. He writes that a woman should dress "as Eve, mourning and repentant, that by every garb of penitence she might the more fully expiate that which she derives from Eve—the ignoring of the first sin, and the odium of human perdition . . . and do you not know that you are an Eve? The sentence of God on this sex of yours lives in this age: the guilt must of necessity live, too."[18]

Another African clergyman, St. Cyril of Alexandria, wrote that ever since Eve every woman is "death's deaconess" and her sex is "especially dishonored" by God and by men (*In Mattheum,* Mt. 28:9). But, on the other hand, "the male sex is ever elect of God, because it is a warrior breed, because it is capable of coming to spiritual vigor, *capable of sowing seed*, of teaching the rest, of tracing its steps to the mature measure of the fullness of Christ [emphasis mine]" (*In Mattheum,* Mt. 14:21).

St. Augustine (d. A.D. 430) regarded sexuality as residing within the animal domain and not properly human at all. He felt that since venereal pleasure is very intense, the sex act is alien to and overwhelms the spirit. Marital intercourse is, therefore, materially evil and is a venial sin. But since woman attracts and arouses man sexually, she is the more guilty party. Again, woman is cast in the role of a temptress, another Eve.

St. Thomas Aquinas, who died in 1274, dominated theology for centuries following his death just as St. Augustine had prevailed in Christianity during the centuries after he died. Their influence on present-day Catholic thinking is still enormous. St. Thomas, following the Greek philosopher Aristotle as well as the thinking of St. Paul and St. Augustine, believed man to be the true human being and woman a misbegotten male. Even though woman is the indispensable partner to man in the work of procreation, she is ontologically inferior and subject to him as to her head.[19] St. Thomas also believed that man's superiority is demonstrated in the act of intercourse since he bears the more active and therefore nobler role, while woman is passive and submissive.[20] Such misunderstandings about embryonic development further strengthened the male sense of superiority. While past ignorance of biology and consequent attitudes are understandable, the continuation of the sexual stereotype of the inferior female, and of woman as "another Eve," with all the implied negative connotations, cannot be easily tolerated. The Church needs a new anthropology that can no longer be the result of the male experience alone, but must well represent both male and female.[21]

Several nontheological factors impinge on the question of women serving in the active ministry. One factor is economic, namely, the availability of jobs. This has been a serious problem among various Protestant denominations—

Episcopal, Lutheran, and Presbyterian, in particular—where there is an ample number of male ministers. Thus, some clergy fear that the ordination of women will create job shortages in some areas. But in Roman Catholicism a serious lack of priests is becoming more obvious with each passing year, and lack of available positions upon ordination does not seem to be a problem for some time to come. In some parishes Catholic nuns are serving virtually as assistant pastors in that they distribute communion, teach courses in Scripture, counsel, and perform other tasks that traditionally have been the duties of the ordained clergy. Such activities promote consciousness-raising, and for many the question inevitably will arise concerning the priesthood of women. If women are capable and accepted in all these pastoral areas, then why are they denied the fullness of the priesthood?

Another factor is sexual. If women are ordained to the priesthood and are celibate and working with male celibate priests, won't this be very tempting? Won't they fall in love and leave the priesthood to get married? Think of the scandal this would cause! But this is to beg the question since a male-dominated Church has already had many defections and scandals. A third factor, and one that cannot easily be ignored, comes from the fact that the Church is international. In the United States there is a strong movement advocating female priests. American women are well-educated and are now accepted in many areas where they were once not permitted, be it in business, politics, or whatever. But this is not the case in Italy, Poland, and many other nations. Their cultures are not so open to women. The question here devolves on whether or not the ordination of female priests would be granted for the universal Church or for particular nations. If granted for the Church in its entirety, then the problems for women in many countries would be insurpassable for some time to come. If granted for particular countries, the result would be more positive. But would the Church ever act in this way? Many think not. A fourth factor is ecumenical. If Rome allows women to be ordained to the priesthood it may jeopardize reunion with the Orthodox, Anglican, and other Christian communions who do not accept the ordination of women into the priesthood. Yet all branches of the Church must be led by the Scriptures and trust in the Holy Spirit for guidance. Reunion can only be valued if it is established on solid foundations. The question of women's ordination cannot be ruled out other than on biblical grounds.

Other objections have been raised, but it seems clear that women must first be given more public roles in the life of the Church so that a fair judgment can be made and prejudices broken down concerning the ordination of women. In fact, education, especially higher education, has allowed women to assume more public roles in society and in the Church. The number of women in professional theological and biblical societies has increased dramatically in recent years. These women are making significant contributions in theological and biblical studies. Other women are assuming responsibilities that were closed to them in the past. Women serve as hospital chaplains, campus ministers, liturgical administrators, religious educators, and occupy a number of other important positions. In priestless parishes, which now total more than 10 percent of all parishes in the United States, women perform the ministries of a pastor with two exceptions. They do not say Mass or hear confessions. These parish administrators conduct Bible studies, counsel, visit the sick, and are the liturgical leaders of the community. In some remote areas women have been commissioned by their bishops to preside at weddings and funerals.

In assuming greater leadership in the Church, women are responding not only to their own calling, but are supported by many official Church documents. As we have seen, *The Decree of the Apostolate of the Laity* of Vatican II states: "Since in our times women have an ever more active share in the whole life of society, it is very important that they participate more widely also in the fields of the Church's apostolate.[22] Earlier, Pope John XXIII said, in *Pacem in Terris* (1963), that women's participation in public life is one of the most significant "signs of the times" to which the Church should attend. And in 1971, the Third World Synod of Bishops called for women to participate in, and share responsibility for, the life of society and of the Church. But the leadership of the Church stops short when the question of ordination arises.

In 1976 the *Declaration on the Question of the Ordination of Women* was issued by the Congregation for the Doctrine of the Faith which presented arguments against the ordination of women to the priesthood. The main arguments given were that the Church is following Jesus, who chose only men as apostles; that it has been the constant tradition of the Church; and that the "natural resemblance" between Christ and the celebrant of the Eucharist would be difficult to see were the role not assumed by a man. The *Declaration* still remains the most basic presentation of the Vatican position. Of course, voluminous responses have been presented to the arguments of the *Declaration.*

In fact the *Declaration* admits that its arguments are not probative. However, it believes that the arguments of those who favor the ordination of women are very speculative and impossible to prove. Because it is a matter of doubt, the *Declaration* says it is better to rely on the tradition itself as most clearly representing the will of God.

In the long run perhaps the most difficult objection to women's ordination—because it is most deeply rooted—is the supposition that in the Bible God has given a blueprint of the Church in which all the basic structures are worked out. Father Raymond Brown describes such an understanding in *Biblical Re-*

flections on Crises Facing the Church. As he notes, such blueprint thinking is not dead, but it has "little scholarly popularity."[23] For those who hold such a view, there can be no ordination of women since this is simply not found in the blueprint. But there is another viewpoint that Brown refers to, for want of a better term, as "in-between ecclesiology."[24] This ecclesiology is somewhere between a blueprint model and an erector-set model. The latter is at the opposite pole from blueprint ecclesiology in that it maintains that Christians are free to go ahead and build the Church as utility directs. Brown sees such erector-set ecclesiology as paying too little heed to the will of Christ, the tradition of the Church, and the guidance of the Holy Spirit. He opts for in-between ecclesiology because it recognizes that history and sociology almost certainly played a role in the development of church structure, especially the pattern of the single bishop and the college of priests surrounding Jesus that had emerged by the end of the first century. The earliest statements about this structure see it as symbolically representing the model of Jesus surrounded by his disciples. Thus the will of Christ has meaning in such ecclesiology, even if the working out of that will is conceived in a more subtle way than is proposed in blueprint ecclesiology.

But precisely because there is no blueprint per se, it is not inconceivable, in view of new historical circumstances, that the Church through in-between ecclesiology can continue its discovery of Christ's will. Such a discovery may imply change and may eventually even lead to the ordination of women as priests.

JESUS AND WOMEN

In order to understand Jesus' attitude toward women and ministry one must recall the manner in which women were treated in first-century Judaism. Women were described in rabbinic literature as temptresses, vain and frivolous. Though not common, polygamy was still permitted during Jesus' lifetime. Male children were viewed as preferable to female children. Every morning Jewish men prayed in thanksgiving to God that they had been created male and not female. Wives were generally confined to the home and in the presence of others they had to cover their heads and wear veils. Women were not permitted to receive any education. Their testimony was not accepted as evidence at court. Legally, women were considered the property of men. In the Jewish religion they were subordinate and silent and were not counted among the *minyan*, the quorum of ten men who had to be present for worship to take place. And the list goes on. In short, it was a man's world.

Despite the strictures of his society, Jesus showed a high regard for women. His preaching revealed a remarkable balance for the concerns of men and women. For example we read:

> The kingdom of heaven is like a mustard seed which a man took and sowed in his field. (Matt. 13:31).
>
> The kingdom of heaven is like yeast a woman took and mixed in with three measures of flour till it was leavened all through. (Mt. 13:33).
>
> Then of two men in the fields one is taken, one left; of two women at the millstone grinding one is taken, one left. (Mt. 24:40–41).

There are many other examples where Jesus addressed women with the same respect and concern he displayed toward men. Women are spiritually akin to Jesus as are men: "Here are my mother and my brothers. Anyone who does the will of my Father in heaven, he is my brother and sister and mother" (Mt. 12:50). Christ performs miracles for women as well as men (see Mt. 8:14–15, 9:24–26, 9:20–22, and 15:22–28). As a matter of fact, in none of Jesus' words and deeds does he give any suggestion that the spiritual potentialities of women are inferior to those of men. And in regard to marriage Jesus boldly stated, "The man who divorces his wife and marries another is guilty of adultery against her" (Mark 10.11). Previously, no one had taught that adultery could be committed against a wife. Adultery was always understood as a crime against the property right of a husband. Jesus' meeting with the Samaritan woman at the well has only recently been understood in all its revolutionary significance. That Jesus spoke to a woman—and a Samaritan at that—in a public place was scandalous. It broke all conventions. Hearing Jesus' message of good news, she hurries to tell it to her fellow townspeople. And Jesus does not prevent her from doing so because she is a woman. It is also clear that certain women were disciples of Jesus, another unusual fact of his ministry. All four evangelists agree that women were the first witnesses to, and first preachers of, the resurrection of Jesus. In other words, Jesus elevated the role of women to an incredibly high degree among his followers.

But did he ordain women to the priesthood? The answer is no. Nor did he ordain men. He called his disciples to follow him and to preach his word. Yet he did not establish structural offices, much less a hierarchy of offices, during his lifetime. As a matter of fact, the Christian priesthood, as we know it today, did not develop until the end of the first century. Scripture scholars and church historians are in general agreement about this fact. There is only one title used in the New Testament to describe the ministry of Jesus' followers before his Resurrection: discipleship. Among his disciples we know there were many women: Mary, his mother; Mary Magdalene; Johanna, the wife of Chuza; Susanna; and others.

In the early years of the Church, observes Elizabeth Tetlow in *Women and Ministry in the New Testament*, "Christians continued to recognize the Jewish priesthood and to participate in temple worship" (see Acts 2:46 and 21:26).[25] Raymond Brown suggests that a Christian priesthood could not develop until the Church had broken off from Judaism and acquired a self-identity as a distinct religion, and until it had developed its own sacrificial cult for which the presence of priests was needed.[26] The first condition occurred after the Temple was destroyed in A.D. 70 and Christianity was banished from the synagogue in A.D. 85. The second condition was met when the Eucharist began to be understood as a cultic sacrifice toward the end of the first century.

The Eucharist had, of course, been instituted by Christ and had been celebrated since early in Christian history by various ministers, especially by those who were disciples, apostles, presbyter-bishops, and presiders at the Eucharist. It was from these offices or ministries that the priesthood eventually emerged. As we have seen women were disciples, and some were most probably "presiders at the Eucharist." Some women were also prophets (1 Cor. 11:5 and Acts 21:9), and prophecy was a liturgical ministry. Prophets presided at eucharistic worship (Acts 13:1–2 and Didache 15:1–2). It is also possible that women were present at the Last Supper, since all four Gospels mention the presence of not only the Twelve but of disciples as well. Disciples was a broader term than just the Twelve and, as we have seen, included some women. Thus, though the early history of eucharistic worship in the Church has remained clouded in obscurity, it is quite possible that women were among the first Christian ministers of the eucharist. This possibility is increased when we realize that there were women missionary apostles, at least in the Pauline churches, and one woman, Junia, is explicitly called an apostle by St. Paul in Romans 16:7.

We can conclude then that in keeping with Jesus' own example of relating to women as persons with the same need of salvation as men and who were equally to be loved and listened to, the early Church gave to women a status unusual for the times. However, two serious questions remain. Why were there only men among the twelve apostles? How can women be priests, "other Christs," since they are obviously female and Jesus was male?

As to why there were only men among the 12 apostles, it seems clear that they had a very specific theological function in the early Church, even though the historical role of the individual members of the Twelve was not very different from that of other apostles. And there were other apostles, including James, Paul, and Barnabas. The Twelve played a special role immediately after the Resurrection. For this reason it was theologically necessary that Matthias be elected to replace Judas. The apostles symbolically represented the twelve tribes of Israel and thus symbolized the completeness of the new people of God at two important moments: at Pentecost, which was the beginning of the Church, and at the eschaton, the Second Coming of Christ, which marked the end of the Church as a historical institution. Once this symbolism had been portrayed at Pentecost, it was no longer necessary that there be twelve historical persons, and so the individual apostles were not replaced after their death. But it was due to this symbolism, the representation of the completeness of Israel, that the members of the Twelve were all men. In Judaism, as we have noted, Israel was legally constituted only by men. The fact that all were male, though important symbolically, had nothing to do with the ministry of the Church. As we have seen, in the earliest Church the roles and functions that later came to be associated with the priestly ministry were never limited to the Twelve. For that matter some functions, such as being administrator of a local church or a leader of public worship, are not explicitly attributed to the Twelve in the New Testament, even though it can be presumed readily that they did, in fact, preside at Eucharist.

The next question pertains to the fact that Jesus was a male. In Roman Catholic symbolism, the priest is referred to as "another Christ." Even though every Christian is called to be another Christ, a priest is believed to represent Christ in a special way as one through whom God communicates grace, particularly sacramental grace, to his people. In Jesus the Word became flesh as a male and so, some will argue, that to truly represent him as "another Christ" one must be male. This was the argument, as we have seen, used in the 1976 Vatican declaration that stated that priests must be male because only males can be the natural signs of Christ. Certainly, since the beginning of the second century, when Christianity adopted the model of the Levitical priesthood from Judaism, this has been the case and has become the tradition in Roman Catholicism. It is well known that the Levitical priesthood was open only to men. But must this be so? And is it not also true that women can be "natural signs of Christ?" Many maintain that the religion of the time and place made it expedient that God become man, not woman. How else could he have been heard? But they go on to add that the symbolism of "another Christ" need not be attached to maleness, but to humanity. As Raymond Brown writes, "If the theology of the priest as another Christ is meant to draw attention to the continued mediatorship of *humanity* in God's giving of grace, one might argue that a priesthood involving both males and females is a better symbol of humanity and overcomes the biological limitation of the incarnation.[27] Were one to accept Fr. Brown's statement, no obstacle would stand in the way of ordaining females from the point of view of sexuality. Nevertheless, it is also not difficult to discern why there is disagreement on the matter, especially from the point of view of tradition. Be that as it may, the executive board of the Catholic Biblical Association of American in a statement entitled *Women and Priestly Ministry: The New Testament Evidence* concludes the section "The Praxis of Jesus and the Apostles" by stating, "Thus, the claim that the intention and example of Jesus and the example of the apostles provide a norm excluding women from priestly ministry cannot be sustained on either logical or historical grounds."[28] And the debate continues.

SUMMARY

Despite the strictures of his society, Jesus showed a high regard for women. There are many examples of Jesus addressing women with the same respect and concern he showed men. His followers were called disciples, and among his disciples there were many women. The priesthood, as we know it today, was not established until toward the end of the first century. The Eucharist had, of course, been instituted by Jesus and had been celebrated since early in Christian history, yet it is possible that women were among the first Christian ministers of the Eucharist.

The reason there were only men among the Twelve is that they had a very special function to perform. The Twelve symbolized the completeness of the new people of God at Pentecost as they will at the Second Coming. In Judaism, Israel was legally constituted only by men. Thus, the fact that all twelve were male, though important symbolically, had nothing per se to do with the ministry of the Church being of necessity male.

In Jesus the Word became flesh as a male and so, some will argue, that to truly represent him as "another Christ" one must be male. The Vatican delcaration of 1976 argued that priests must be male because only males can be natural signs of Christ. Many maintain that the religion of Jesus' time made it expedient that God became male not female. But they go on to add that the symbolism of "another Christ" need not be attached to maleness but should be broadened to include all humanity. Raymond Brown writes that one might argue that a priesthood involving both males and females is a better symbol of humanity and overcomes the biological limitations of the Incarnation.

ST. PAUL: WOMEN AND MINISTRY

The picture of the ministry of women that emerges both from the Acts of the Apostles and from most of the Pauline epistles is of women fully accepted by the Christian community, laboring side by side on an equal footing with men in the work of spreading the Gospel. Men certainly predominated, as would be expected in the culture of the day, but women were given a status in the

Church quite unusual for the times. In the New Testament there were not ministries of men or ministries of women but rather only ministries of Jesus in which both men and women served. Generally speaking, Christian ministry in the New Testament is ministry of service. There were apostles, prophets, teachers, evangelists, and deacons, and all served the Church, each with his or her own gifts, for the building up of the Christian community. As we have seen, the exclusion of women came only toward the end of the first century when the office of priesthood formally was instituted and was modeled on the Levitical priesthood of the Old Testament. This was clearly a postbiblical development.

When reading the epistles of St. Paul, one is struck by the role women played. Their names are well known: Phoebe, Lydia, Synteche, Evodia, Priscilla, and Eunice, among others. But the same Paul who praises these women placed restrictions on the women of Corinth because of their exuberance in their new-found freedom in the Lord. Paul felt that they were departing too much from the cultural norm. The restrictions in 1st Corinthians and 1st Timothy have burdened women to the present time and have barred women from any effective participation in the decision-making processes in the Church. And yet it is important to note that in the New Testament there are no texts that address the specific question of women and Church office. Only three epistolary passages deal with women in the assembly (1 Cor. 11:36; 14:33a–35; 1 Tim. 2:11–15), and these are simply disciplinary regulations pertaining to proper conduct. The exclusion of women from Church office cannot be deduced from these texts.

In 1st Corinthians 11:36, Paul instructs women to wear a headdress, which was the customary attire when praying or prophesying, so that they would not appear eccentric or cause scandal. Even though Paul attempts to ground this regulation in the order of creation, the Church has acknowledged the cultural contingency of the regulation by no longer imposing the rule. Paul's motivation in laying down this code is understood as disciplinary, not dogmatic. He is speaking of a particular situation in a particular time and place. In 1 Cor. 14:33a–35, women are forbidden to speak in the assembly. The verb used is *lalein*, which means "to speak." It is incorrect to translate *lalein* as meaning "to teach" and to use this verse as though it means women are forbidden from the official function of teaching. Such an interpretation is unwarranted by the text and the context. Rather the context indicates the prohibition is against asking questions (v. 35) or in some way disturbing the assembly (vs. 28, 30). It is in the First Letter to Timothy, a pastoral epistle that is generally assumed to have been written in a later period, where women are admonished not "to teach" (*didaskein*) but to be submissive and silent (1 Tim. 2:11–15). That this is not a universal principle is clear since women in Paul's churches not only prayed and prophesied at worship (1 Cor. 11:5) but also exercised the ministry of teaching (Acts 18:26). If the command for silence were to be taken literally here, then should we not also accept as literal the stern orders given by Paul that women are not to wear braided hair, gold, pearls, or expensive clothes (1 Tim. 2:9)? It seems clear, then, that these three passages, which limit women's role to what is decent and customary, are pastoral regulations motivated by the social and cultural factors of Paul's day and cannot be taken as universal theological laws relating to ministry in the Church.

CONCLUSION

An examination of the biblical evidence in the New Testament indicates that women exercised roles and functions that later were associated with priestly ministry. The arguments against the ordination of women to the priesthood based on the practice of Jesus and the Apostles, St. Paul, and the early Church do not seem to be absolute. The evidence, even though not decisive by itself, does seem to many to point toward the ordination of women. The crux of the problem, as indicated earlier, lies in the interpretation of Scripture. The study of Scripture is a developing science, and current biblical scholarship is in the process of rediscovering the prominent role of women in ministry in the New Testament. New discoveries in this area, as have occurred in other areas of biblical scholarship in the past, may eventually bring about a change in the Church's position. But for the immediate future there seems to be little realistic hope for the ordination of women to the priesthood. The Church has evolved in new directions many times in the past under the guidance of the Holy Spirit. As women continue to serve the Church so positively in a variety of new ministries, the stimulus for change may well be provided.

Chapter Six

Hispanic Theology and Spirituality in the United States

The American hierarchy is conscious of the rising importance of the Hispanic population who are projected to constitute the largest percentage of U.S. Catholics in the next two decades. The word *Hispanic* is used in this book to cover a variety of Spanish-speaking national groups, including Mexican Americans, Puerto Ricans, Cubans, Dominicans, and Central and South Americans. Currently the Hispanic population in the United States is estimated at 36 million, of which the largest group is of Mexican origin, followed by Puerto Ricans and Cubans. Anywhere from a low of 75 percent to a high of 95 percent of the Hispanic population is estimated to be baptized Catholics.

In an effort to make better known the life of Hispanic Catholics, Moises Sandoval has written an excellent book, *On the Move: A History of the Hispanic Church in the United States*.[1] The Hispanic population, because of its number, may well give a particular character to the Catholic Church in the United States in the twenty-first century, just as European immigrants gave their particular character to the Church during the nineteenth and twentieth centuries.

The definitive statement of the policy of the Church in relation to Hispanics and their inculturation was published by the American bishops in a pastoral letter in 1983, *The Hispanic Presence: Challenge and Commitment*, followed in 1987 by another pastoral letter, *National Plan for Hispanic Ministry*.[2] I will concentrate on the 1983 letter, which is the basis of the bishops' policy. The letter describes the social, cultural, and religious situation of Hispanics in the United States. The bishops are well aware that Hispanics come from a culture that has been penetrated by the Catholic faith, but in a very different way from that of European Catholics. They are also cognizant that Hispanics are among the poorest people in the United States, whereas

Catholics in general are middle class. It is difficult to bridge the gap across cultures and even more difficult to bridge the gap across social class. This complicates the problem of inculturation, as does the fact that, unlike Europeans in the past, Hispanics have come to the United States largely without their own clergy.

In *The Hispanic Presence* the bishops outline the challenge to the Church in terms of ministry and response to the social, economic, and political needs of the Hispanics and make a commitment to provide whatever resources are needed to help them realize their full potential as vital contributors of the Catholic experience in the United States. An important feature of the letter is the firm commitment to a policy of cultural pluralism in the United States and of religious pluralism within the Catholic Church. The letter also discusses the poverty of Hispanics, and though it is not presented as a problem of difference of social class, the letter calls for a "preferential option for the poor" and asks that the Church be a strong advocate of the poor. The bishops describe Hispanic culture as an experience in which "faith and life are inseparable." The Spanish colonial experience brought about a distinct culture penetrated by the Catholic faith, which in turn became the cultural support of the faith. This is different from the religious experience of life in the United States, which generally is lived in a secular culture:

> As with many nationalities with strong Catholic traditions, religion and culture, faith and life are inseparable for Hispanics. Hispanic Catholicism is an outstanding example of how the Gospel can permeate a culture even to its roots.[3]

In coming to the United States Hispanics face, on the level of everyday living, a clash of cultures that can be upsetting and even traumatic. In great measure this occurs because of the conflict between the highly individualistic and competitive culture of the United States and the personalistic and family-oriented culture of Hispanic countries. Tension also occurs between the Hispanic style of Catholic life and practice and the style practiced by the Church in the United States. These differences of style can lead to misunderstanding and tension. Central to this issue is the fact that Hispanics are calling for a cultural pluralism that would permit the continuation of Hispanic language and culture in the process of their adjustment to the United States. In response to this problem, the bishops wrote,

> The pastoral needs of Hispanic Catholics are indeed great; although their faith is deep and strong, it is being challenged and eroded by steady social pressures to assimilate.
>
> Respect for culture is rooted in the dignity of people made in God's image. The Church shows its esteem for their dignity by working to ensure that pluralism, not

assimilation and uniformity, is the guiding principle in the life of communities in both ecclesial and secular societies.[4]

One of the problems Hispanics face when they emigrate to the United States results from the fact that in their homelands their faith was supported by their culture, even in the absence of clergy and religious instruction. Because of this the change of religious environment is a profound shock to them, and the adjustment to a new culture is difficult. This problem is compounded by the fact that Hispanics are the first Catholic immigrants to come to the United States in large numbers without a native clergy to accompany them. Earlier immigrants had many of their own clergy and religious priests and nuns with them, and this allowed for a perpetuation of their culture. The Hispanic clergy are not sufficient in number, generally speaking, to allow them to accompany their countrypeople to the United States.

The lack of Hispanic clergy has presented a great challenge to the clergy of the United States. Thousands of American priests and religious personnel have learned to speak Spanish and to understand the Hispanic culture to prepare themselves to minister to the newly arriving Hispanics. This response has been admirable though inadequate. Centers have been established to prepare Americans for Hispanic ministry. The Mexican American Cultural Center established by Father Virgil Elizondo in San Antonio, Texas, has made a remarkable contribution in this regard.

One of the serious concerns of the Church is the small number of Hispanics aspiring to the priesthood and the religious life in the United States. Because vocations to the priesthood were never numerous in Latin America, there is no tradition on which to build. Added to this is the drop in vocations worldwide. Most dioceses in which Hispanics are numerous have established an Office of Hispanic Ministry. And many Hispanics have been active in their response to life in the Church in the United States. The Cursillo Movement is very popular, for example. It is a brief retreat designed to bring about a deep conversion of the individual, which is followed up by regular meetings to keep the experience alive. The charismatic movement and the Christian Family Movement are also widespread.

One of the most difficult questions facing the contemporary Catholic Church in America is the assimilation of Hispanics into American society. An important study of this issue was done in 1980 by A.J. Jaffe, Ruth M. Cullen, and Thomas D. Boswell, *The Changing Demography of Spanish Americans*.[5] They found among Hispanics a consistent pattern of assimilation similar to that of earlier ethnic groups. Using the indicators of language, socioeconomic levels, fertility, and intermarriage of Hispanics with other ethnic groups, Jaffe and his group found evidence of a trend toward adopting the dominant cultural patterns of the United States: English becomes the language of common usage; socioeconomic advancement improves in the second and third generations and with the number of years in the United States; fertility declines with education. The pace at which this convergence is taking place differs for each Hispanic group and differs within each group, of course. But the evidence of a trend toward convergence is consistent. The Jaffe group concludes their study this way:

> The Spanish-American groups in the United States . . . have changed and will continue to change in a manner paralleling the general society. . . . With each passing decade, they are being brought closer to the mainstream of social change and economic development of the larger society until eventually there will be a merging . . . in another generation or two they will be almost indistinguishable from the general U.S. population.[6]

The standard sociological indicators, therefore, lead to the conclusion that the experience of the Hispanics will be similar to that of previous immigrant groups. However, there are some notable differences today that may result in a retention of Hispanic culture. Hispanics come from "next door," from Cuba, the Dominican Republic, Puerto Rico, Mexico, and Central and South America. Mexico borders the United States, and Central America can be reached by land. Both the proximity and the ease of travel back and forth reinforces an already deeply rooted culture. At the same time, the increasing emphasis on cultural pluralism in the United States has created a climate much more favorable to the retention of a native culture than was the case with earlier immigrants. Added to this, the strong emphasis by Hispanics on bilingual and bicultural programs in the public schools reflect their strong sense of culture and a determination to perpetuate it.

Hispanics are not alone in attempting to retain their culture. This is certainly true of African Americans as well as others who celebrate their ethnicity in festivals, neighborhood parties, and in literature and dance. There are many reasons given for this recapturing of cultural roots, one of the most prominent of which is an effort to retain supports for self-identity in a world marked by uncertainty and rapid change. Among the Hispanics, cultural adaptation to the United States is taking place as it has for all previous ethnic groups within the second and subsequent generations that achieve a new cultural understanding, one that hopefully is a dynamic blend of Hispanic and American influence. As a consequence the twenty-first century may witness a new life radiating from the Hispanic community, which will have a significant impact on the Church, liturgically and theologically, and in many areas pertaining to social justice.

Peter C. Phan, in his essay "Contemporary Theology and Inculturation," gives an excellent overview of the development of Hispanic theology, which I will summarize.[7] One important event in the development of Hispanic theology was the founding of the Academy of Catholic Hispanic Theologians of the United States (ACHTUS) in 1988. The Academy includes male and female theologians. It has deliberately differentiated U.S. Hispanic theologians from Latin American liberation theology, even though they have much in common, because the purpose of the Academy is to concentrate on problems unique to the United States. The Academy also endorses ecumenical dialogue with Hispanic Protestant theologians. This is being done with a Protestant group, La Communidad, and *Apuntes*, until recently the only journal of Hispanic theology in the United States. In October 1993, the Academy began publishing its own quarterly journal, *Journal of Hispanic/Latino Theology*.

Fr. Virgil Elizando, a priest of the Archdiocese of San Antonio, Texas, is seen as the first contemporary U.S. Hispanic theologian. From the late 1960s to the late 1980s he was the sole, highly visible U.S. Hispanic theologian. He is a prolific and internationally known theologian, and he is now followed by a new generation of well-trained and well-published theologians who are dedicated to developing a distinctive Hispanic theology that is contextualized into the cultural situation of the United States.

Hispanic theology begins with a cultural and social analysis of the Hispanic community in the United States. Elizando, both in *The Galilean Journey* and in his article "Mestizaje as a Locus of Theological Reflection," writes that U.S. Hispanics are characterized by what he terms *Mestizaje*.[8] Mestizaje does not simply refer to the psysiological fact that Hispanics, like many other peoples, are a mixed race composed of many bloods. Rather, it refers to the violent forging of a new people from the sexual intercourse that occurred between the Spanish Conquistadores and the vanquished Amerindian women. *Mestizaje* also refers to the subjugation of the Amerindian religion by medieval Roman Catholicism. Because of this double conquest, the *mestizos* are forced to live as foreigners on their own land. As Elizando puts it, Mexican Americans suffer from an unfinished or undefined identity. Their Spanish is too Anglicized for the Mexicans, and their English too Mexicanized for the Anglo Americans. For Mexicans, Hispanics are too close to the United States, and for Anglo Americans they are too close to Mexico. The *mestizo* reality is feared and rejected by both racial groups that produce it because it blurs the identity-constituting boundaries between them. This is the peculiar situation of U.S. Hispanics, which Elizando describes with the term *el rechazo* (rejection). The combined character of "Mexican American" cannot be adequately understood by an analysis of either group. Elizando maintains that *mestizaje* is a symbol of biological-cultural oppression, exploitation, and alienation. However, and this is most important, this symbol contains a seed for creating a new reality and a new culture, provided it is not reabsorbed into either of the cultures that produced it. Thus *mestizaje* is a starting point for U.S. Hispanic theology.

Hispanic theology is deeply rooted in the Hispanic experience of Church rather than from a somewhat removed academic mindset. It is a Church experience that is strongly sacramental but steeped in popular devotions. It also tends to be nonclerical. As Phan writes,

> Indeed, one of the distinctive features of the Hispanic church is that since its beginnings it developed in spite of the scarcity of priests. The laity has always exercised a key role in the life of the Church: *sacristans* who functioned as parish administrators, *rezadores* [prayer leaders] who led funeral prayers, *mayordomos* [stewards] who were in charge of parish finances, and *catechists* responsible for religious instruction.[9]

Because Hispanic theology is rooted in the Hispanics' experience of *mestizaje* and *rechazo* and is in solidarity with them, it must begin with the existential option for the poor. This means that central to its methodology is the relation between theory and practice. Robert Goizueto, who has written extensively on this issue, warns U.S. Hispanic theologians not to yield to the antiintellectual temptation of renouncing theory in favor of practice. He also cautions them not to follow postmodernity's premature rejection of the Enlightenment's demand for rationality. This might lead to the marginalization of Hispanic theology by Anglo theologians as no more than "Hispanic advocacy theology," which could perhaps be judged as devoid of intellectual rigor and therefore irrelevant to the theological enterprise.[10]

From its very beginning the Academy of Catholic Hispanic Theologians of the United States has sought to recognize the work of Hispanic female theologians. Approximately 25 percent of U.S. Hispanic theologians are women. They are in the process of developing a *mujerista* theology—a theology that has as its point of departure the experience of Hispanic American women in the dominant Anglo Saxon culture, facing oppression and discrimination from both a sexist world as women and a racist world as Hispanics.

Hispanic Americans come from different countries and from different social backgrounds as has been noted. They have been influenced by many cultural factors and by indigenous religious beliefs and practices which in turn have been affected by social, educational, and secular influences of the North American culture and various Christian movements throughout the history of the United States. It is helpful to note that no other European culture has been in this country longer than the Hispanic. They were already in the Southeast and Southwest by the late 16th century. In more recent times a steady influx of Hispanic immigrants has increased their visibility. It is clear that in the future the Hispanic population will play an ever more powerful role both in the wider society and in the development of the Catholic Church.

Hispanic Catholics are extremely diverse. They come from 19 different Latin American nations, from the Caribbean and from Spain. The largest group as noted previously are the Mexican-Americans, followed by Puerto-Ricans and Cubans. The Dominican Republic, Peru, Ecuador, Chile and increasingly Central America, especially El Salvador, as well as other Latin American countries, are well represented. Hispanics vary in their racial origins, color, history, achievements, and expressions of faith. However, they share many elements of culture including a deeply rooted Catholicism, commitment to the extended family, and a common language, Spanish, spoken with different accents. They are found in every state and in nearly every diocese. Many, especially in the Southwest, live in rural areas, but over 85 percent live in large urban centers like Chicago, New York, Los Angeles, Miami, San Francisco and San Antonio.

For Hispanics, life is seen as sacred and filled with the presence of God. With the arrival of the Spaniards in America in the 16th century there began an encounter between two different worlds with their own religious views and culture. The Spanish brought with them a national, hierarchical and sacramental Catholicism which would transform, though not completely, the mythic, oral, collective and symbolic indigenous religious culture. In succeeding generations German Martinez observes:

> . . . European missionaries—mainly Franciscans, Augustinians, Dominicans, followed by the Jesuits—brought to America a Catholicism of sacramental practice, popular devotion, communal participation, dramatic expression, and ascetic and mystical idealism. The Spanish humanism and mysticism of the Catholic Reformation blended with the strong indigenous piety in the newly discovered lands. (The Spanish mysticism of Teresa of Avila and John of the Cross is well known). . . . The process of sacramentalization, pious devotions, festive celebrations, and dramatic plays based on Jesus' life and sufferings flourished.[11]

Hispanic-American spirituality is personal and communal, sacramental, and popular. Great value is placed on interpersonal relationships within the family and society. Traditionally, the family more than the parish has been the center of Hispanic spirituality and religious traditions. As Martinez writes:

> . . . the sense of the sacred in life and of the divine presence in it calls for festive ritual expressions, which form an integral part of Hispanic-American religious life, despite the modern Anglo-American environment of secularization. The *sensus fidei* is lived creatively and reverently in ways well beyond the Catholic sacraments and is expressed not only in church but at home and in the

streets. Traditionally, faith and life have been inseparable in this rich religious-cultural heritage. Art and folklore, processions and festivals, especially in veneration of saints and in the celebration of Christmas-Epiphany, with its pageants and *pastorelas*, and of Holy Week, with its dramas of Christ's passion, have been important components of rituals for the people.[12]

Within this fervent popular piety, adoration of Christ and veneration of the Blessed Virgin Mary are preeminent in Hispanic-American spirituality. Christ is worshipped under many titles, but perhaps most especially as Savior and Suffering Servant. Identifying with the crucified Christ has a strong appeal since his suffering mirrors their own rejection as a migrant and often marginalized people. Devotion to Mary as the Mother of Jesus is celebrated by the various Hispanic nationalities in a number of ways. Most notable is the feast of Our Lady of Guadalupe. The Guadalupe event is a powerful symbol, "not only of religious faith and spirituality, but also of human liberation and new life in the history of the Mexican people and in the lives of many Hispanic Americans.[13] A national feast in honor of Our Lady of Guadalupe was approved for the United States in 1988.

In order to preserve the richness of this spiritual life and cultural values, pastoral strategies must be clear and well directed. Among the greatest concerns are the secularized environment in the United States, lack of adequate Christian education, and unwelcoming attitudes in a number of parishes. Allan Figueroa Deck, S.J., in an article in *America* entitled "Proselytism and Hispanic Catholics: How Long Can We Cry Wolf?" addresses the problem of faithfully serving the needs of Hispanic-Americans.[14] After noting the defection of large numbers of Hispanics to other religious denominations, he points out that the regular Catholic parish system is inadequate to deal with the problem. Generally speaking parishes are too large. Achieving an environment that is welcoming and familiar is extremely hard to maintain in the large, urban, ethnically-mixed parish. Hispanics are attracted to small faith-sharing groups. As Deck notes:

"No matter how accepting and receptive the parish might be to Hispanics (unfortunately, there are still many that are not), its *modus operandi* is often out of gear with the dispositions and needs of Hispanics, especially the immigrants whose status in U.S. society is still so precarious."[15] He goes on to say that second-generation Hispanics usually speak English but in other respects are very Hispanic. He believes that mainstreaming them to the standard Anglo—or integrated parish community—often does not work. What is needed are priests and other pastoral associates who are capable of reaching out to the people in their own language and in ways consistent with their Catholic heritage.

Deck then discusses what he has observed to be the three pastoral approaches in serving Hispanics. He characterizes them as: 1) sacramentalist, 2) reformist, 3) liberationist. None of these approaches is necessarily bad, they simply are inadequate in his opinion.

The sacramentalist approach simply provides the eucharistic liturgies, confessions, and a few popular devotions for the people with a catechesis that merely reinforces the sacramental encounters. All this is necessary but the people need more. What is needed as well is personal attention, adult education, and a more intimate sense of Christian community. Nevertheless the sacramentalist approach is the logical place to begin. It has the advantage of resembling what the people have known in their native countries.

The second approach, the reformist, is common enough in the church in the United States. It attempts to implement Vatican II which in the United States "means making the Catholic faith more explicit, more articulate and more a matter of personal commitment."[16] Deck understands that this approach is at home in the environment of a modern, secularized nation such as the United States, "but it is still far from the mainstream of Hispanic Catholicism."[17] He maintains that U.S. Catholicism is very uncomfortable with the cultural core of Hispanic Catholicism: popular religiosity. "It views all of that as at best quaint and at worst superstitious."[18] He adds that the reformist approach is generally the pastoral orientation of the Catholic Church in the United States and that this approach mixes with Hispanic spirituality like oil and water.

The third approach is liberationist which is concerned with raising the socioeconomic and political awareness of the poor. Deck writes of this approach: "Sacramental concerns, popular piety and Vatican II are left in the dust. The oppression that has characterized the life of Hispanics must be resisted. Everything else in the life of the church is secondary. Such an approach, however, is not readily comprehensible to the ordinary Hispanic, for whom the conscious admixture of social awareness, politics and Christian life is still unfamiliar."[19] Though Deck seems to have understated the meaning of the liberationist approach, his point is well taken.

Deck feels that none of the above approaches are per se unacceptable. But what is most important for Hispanics involves creating liturgies which meet the needs of Hispanics as well as the fostering of small faith-sharing groups. As for liturgies as applied to Hispanics, provisions for Spanish and bilingual worship is necessary according to the traditions and customs of the people being served. The presence of Hispanic liturgists on parish and diocesan councils is essential as is the celebration of traditional feasts and special occasions. The choice of liturgical art, gestures, and music combined with a spirit of hospitality can create an inviting environment. With regard to faith-sharing groups two of the most successful forms of outreach to Hispanics have been the charismatic renewal and the Cursillo Movement. Both of these approaches stress affectivity and peer testimony which have strong appeal to Hispanics. Hispanic family celebrations such as baptisms, *quinceañeras*, weddings, anniversaries, *fiestas patrias*, *novenarios, velorios*, and funerals also provide marvelous opportunities for evangelization and for the development of Hispanic spirituality. The American bishops have been very supportive in addressing the needs of Hispanics. It is up to the individual parishes to address the needs of Hispanics in their congregations. And although Deck wrote in 1988, what he has to say is still very relevant. Some progress has been made but the Church still has much work to do in reaching out to its Hispanic brothers and sisters.

Chapter Seven

African-American Theology and Spirituality

The term African-American began to be used in the decade of the 1980s to replace the term "Black" which had been used since the 1960s as the result of a newly discovered pride in racial and cultural consciousness. The term "Black" is global and refers to all those of African heritage.

African-American Roman Catholics number somewhere between 2.3 million and 3 million of an estimated 67 million Roman Catholics in the United States. The worldwide population of Roman Catholics who are African (Continental Africans) or of African descent, i.e., Africans who were enslaved or migrated to the Caribbean, Europe, the United States, South America and elsewhere numbers about 200 million.

The earliest record of a Black Catholic community in this country is found in the parish register of the oldest Spanish colonial settlement in the United States dating to 1565, namely, the Spanish colonial settlement in St. Augustine, Florida. And although the presence of Black Catholics in the colonies had been documented in the 16th century, it wasn't until the period following the Civil War that the bishops of the United States explored the question of expanding a Catholic mission among the emancipated slaves. In 1886 Augustus Tolton was ordained in Rome (since no seminary in this country would accept him) and sent to work in the United States. He is recognized as the first African-American priest in this country. In 1888 John R. Slattery, an Irish Catholic Mill Hill missionary, opened St. Joseph's seminary in Baltimore to train Black and White men for the priesthood and to work among African-Americans.

In 1829 the first successful foundation of a community of Black religious women was the Oblate Sisters of Providence in Baltimore, Maryland. And in 1842 Henriette Delisle founded the Sisters of the Holy Family in New Orleans. Their mission was to care for the sick and orphans and to provide education for girls from the families of free Blacks. The third community of Black sisters, the Franciscan Handmaids of Mary, was founded in 1916 in Savannah, Georgia.

To adequately understand African-American Roman Catholic spirituality it is necessary to have some understanding of African spirituality. Before the Second Vatican Council the official position of the Catholic Church regarding the values of African religion was not positive. The rich religious reality of African culture was simply not understood. However, Catholic African theologians helped the Church overcome this problem. They prepared the way for the first official statement from Rome which acknowledged some of the essential features of African spirituality. This occurred in Pope Paul VI's message to the people of Africa, *Africae Terrarum*, in 1967, in which he recognized their unique spiritual heritage as worthy of respect and valuable for the Church.

Chris Nwaka Egbulem, O.P., in an article "African Spirituality" which appears in *The New Dictionary of Catholic Spirituality* delineates seven concepts which he believes can be considered to be the pillars of African life and the essence of African spirituality.[1] These concepts are as follows:

1) *The active presence of the Creator God in the world*—African spirituality gives a prominent place to the Creator God as Father and Mother, present, alive, active, and in direct communication and collaboration with creation. All that exists has its origin and meaning with God and will terminate in God.

2) *A unified sense of reality*—For the African, divinity and humanity are not seen in isolation. The sacred and the profane interact. Just as the body is united to the soul, divinity indwells our world.

3) *Life as the ultimate gift*—African spirituality identifies life as the primary gift of the Creator to the creature. It is to be received gratefully, sustained, enhanced, and safeguarded. Life at all levels is sacred.

4) *The family and community as the place to be born, live, and die*—A vital link exists between an individual and members of the same family, clan, or community. A person's identification with their family and community determines the nature of their existence and survival. This is equally true of men and women.

5) *The active role of ancestors*—Ancestors are those members of the family or community whose lives have left a great heritage to the living and who continue to influence their families from beyond the visible world. They are intermediaries between God and the people. The cult of ancestors in African life somewhat resembles the communion of saints in Roman

Catholic spirituality. In fact, for the first time in the history of Roman Catholicism the invocation of African ancestors in the liturgy was approved in the new Liturgy of the Eucharist in Zaire (*Missel romain pour les diocéses du Zaire*,1988).

6) *The sense of oral tradition*—The spoken word has great power in African spirituality. The word in African thought encompasses the entire system of communication. This is what is generally referred to as oral tradition in African life and it includes communication in music, song, dance, poetry, proverbs, storytelling, art, and ritual. Prayer involves all of these.

7) *The sacredness of nature and the environment*—Africans see the presence of the divine in creation. Created nature and the human environment, visible and invisible, bear the mark of goodness and godliness.

And as Jamie Phelps, O.P., remarks:

> It should be apparent that black spirituality transcends and crosses denominational and ecclesial boundaries. Its characteristic cultural expressions are more evident in some congregations and denominations than in others; consequently, it is more or less empirically evident in the lives of individual black Christians.[2]

In their pastoral letter, *What We Have Seen and Heard* (1984), the ten Black Catholic bishops of the United States suggested four major gifts, rooted in their African heritage, that Black Catholics are called upon to share within the Black community at large and within the Church. These gifts are mentioned in *What We Have Seen and Heard*, a Pastoral Letter on Evangelization from the Black Bishops of the United States.[3]

First, African-American spirituality is Scripture based for both Black Catholics and Black Protestants. The starting point of the sermon is always the Word of God. The point of the Black church's biblically centered approach is to hear God's word from the past as it is evidenced in the present. Often the preaching is dialogical with the congregation affirming the preacher by nods of the head, amens, applause, and the like. Also, as Jamie Phelps notes, "The preaching and singing is necessarily emotional, because the worshippers have been touched at the core of their being, moved by the presence of the Spirit deep in their soul."[4] The bishops urge their fellow Black Catholics to share their love of Scripture.

The next gift mentioned in the pastoral letter is the message of liberation, of freedom. The bishops state that Black people know what freedom is because they remember the dehumanizing force of slavery, racist prejudice and oppression. This understanding of freedom brings responsibility and must be shared with the whole church. It is necessary to oppose all social injustice, all discrimination, and all violence wherever it may appear.

The third gift described by the bishops is that of reconciliation which is the fruit of liberation. True reconciliation arises only where there is mutually perceived equality. Here the question centers on cultural identity and cultural values. A people must safeguard their own cultural identity and their own cultural values and must respect others and their cultural values. The bishops teach that Black Catholics should be an agent of change in working toward mutual respect and true justice not only in the United States but throughout the world as well.

Finally, the bishops suggest four major characteristics of black spirituality.

1) Black spirituality is contemplative. Every place is a place for prayer because God's presence is heard and felt everywhere. Black spirituality senses the awe of God's transcendence and the intimacy of his presence. As Jamie Phelps writes:

> Any person born into the religious tradition of African or African Diaspora cultures is nurtured from birth into a style of life that witnesses to the belief that God is manifest everywhere and in every person, thing, or event.[5]

2) Black spirituality is holistic. Religious experience is an experience of the whole person—this includes one's emotions and intellect, the heart as well as the head. The bishops maintain that divisions between intellect and emotion, spirit and body, action and contemplation, individual and community, sacred and secular are foreign to the African heritage.

3) Joy is a gift and a hallmark of Black spirituality. Joy is first of all celebration and celebration is movement and song, rhythm and song, color and sensation, exultation and thanksgiving. This joy is a sign of faith and of hope and trust in God's promises. It is a reaction to God's word. The bishops teach that a joyful person is troubled by the sight of another's sadness and seeks to console and encourage. This is a gift that must be shared.

4) The sense of community is a major component of Black spirituality. In African culture individual identity is to be found within the context of the community. This communal sense is a gift to be shared in a society which is individualistic such as is evident in the United States. This communal dimension is evident in liturgy. Worship is always a community celebration. The sense of community is always present in working for social justice.

The communal dimension of Black spirituality permeates liturgy and worship. Worship must be shared. One prays and acts within and for community.

Music in the Black religious tradition is essential. As William B. McClain observes, the Negro spirituals that speak of life and death, suffering and sorrow, love and judgment, grace and hope, justice and mercy, were born out of the tradition of slavery. He writes: "These songs are timeless—the work of ages. They tell of exile and trouble, of strife and hiding; they grope toward some unseen power and sigh for rest in the end."[6] W.E.B. DuBois points out in *The Souls of Black Folks*, "But through the sorrow of the sorrow songs there breathes a hope—a faith in the ultimate justice of things."[7] John Wesley Works' comment on the Negro spiritual is insightful. In his book, *Folk Songs of the American Negro*, he writes:

> To our fathers who came out of bondage and who are still with us, these songs are prayers, praises and sermons. They sang them at work; in leisure moments; they crooned them to their babes in the cradles; to their wayward children; they sang them to the sick, wracked with pain on beds of affliction; they sang them over their dead. Blessings, warnings, benedictions and the very heartbeats of life were all expressed to our fathers by their songs.[8]

William B. McClain notes that another musical genre, the gospel song, was created in the North and became the Northern urban counterpart of the Negro spirituals of the South. The gospel song arose in the midst of the early exodus from the farms and hamlets of the South, when Blacks arrived in Chicago, New York, Detroit and other northern cities, and found themselves in a strange land. McClain writes:

> These songs of hope and promise have helped to bring a people through the torture chambers of the last two centuries. The music of the black religious tradition has affirmed that just being alive is good and worth celebrating and singing and shouting about. That music has nourished the black community. It has soothed its hurts, sustained its hopes, and bound its wounds.[9]

The creative genius of Reverend Clarence Joseph Rivers led the National Office for Black Catholics to conduct workshops on liturgical adaptations to Black culture. Father Rivers emerged in the 1960s as an advocate of adapting Catholic worship to African-American culture. He introduced the melodies, harmonies, symbols and rituals of African American Sacred Song into Roman Catholic worship. In the decade of the 1970s African-American Catholics continued to adapt their worship to their African-American culture. They introduced elements of their African-American culture such as spirituals, spontaneity and emotive expressions into their Sunday liturgies. Gospel choirs became popular. These efforts laid the groundwork for the 1987 publication of *Lead Me, Guide Me: The African American Catholic Hymnal*.[10] In 1989 the bishops' committee on Black liturgy published *Plenty Good Room: The Spirit and Truth of African American Catholic Worship.*[11] Concerning this document Jay P. Dolan remarks that it is "a substantive essay" and it offered "a solid explanation of the principle of cultural adaptation in the liturgy and how the application of this principle could lead to an authentic African-American Catholic worship."[12]

In the practice of their faith social concern and social justice are critical to Black Catholics. This is not surprising since as a people they have known and continue to experience racial and economic oppression. In 1979, encouraged by its Black members, the Catholic bishops issued a pastoral letter condemning racism, *Brothers and Sisters to Us: U.S. Bishops Pastoral on Racism in Our Day.*[13]

As for theology, M. Shawn Copeland's article, "African American Catholics and Black Theology: An Interpretation," gives an account of the development of the 20th century Black Catholic movement and the contributions of selected writers in the fields of theology, liturgy, and pastoral ministry.[14] Black theological voices have been absent in the Catholic church in the United States until the reforms of Vatican II and the Civil Rights Movement in the 1960s. Black Catholic scholars, male and female, continue to be few today, but their voices are beginning to be heard. Tragically, two of the leading Black Catholic scholars died before they were able to present their theological perspectives in a systematic form. Father Bede Abrams, O.F.M.Com., and Father Joseph Nearon, S.S.S., can be said to be the founding fathers of Black Catholic theology. Together with Sister Thea Bowman they were responsible for the establishment and staffing of the Institute for Black Catholic Studies, a summer graduate program at Xavier University in New Orleans, the only Black Catholic University in the United States. They mentored many of those who are emerging as Black Catholic scholars today.

Black Catholic theologians analyze what is distinctive about Black Catholicism, exploring their African roots as expressed in their celebration of Christ in song and word. And as Diana Hayes writes:

> They also seek an appreciation of the importance of both scripture and tradition intertwined with an emphasis on a sacramentality that is Catholic in its foundation but Black in its expression. Black Catholics in the United States share the tradition of the church from its earliest beginnings, but they also bring a critique of that tradition, serving as a "subversive memory" within the church itself. They call the church to live up to its proclamation of scriptures that reveal God's consistent option for the poor and the oppressed, scriptures that have been too often submerged by a praxis that ignored the plight of those same poor and oppressed.[15]

M. Shawn Copeland in an article "Foundation for Catholic Theology in an African American Context" lists seven features of Black Catholic Theology.[16]

1) This theology will recognize and acknowledge 'black religious experience' as the critical locus and resource for theologizing.
2) This theology will affirm and sustain black humanity and, at the same time, affirm the dignity and grandeur *of all human life* as it comes from the hand of God.
3) This theology will strive to articulate and to mediate an understanding of the world of God from *within* and for the compound—complexity of black or African-American culture. It will aim at a basic liberation of all human subjects.
4) A Catholic theological mediation in African American perspective will aim for creative and autonomous thematization: one that recovers *from within* African American culture, the signs, symbols, and images of religious experience and consciousness; that expresses black peoples' peculiar saving encounter with the Triune God and that challenges black peoples' faith in relation to a praxis which measures itself by the praxis of Jesus; and that understands and responds aggressively to black peoples' complex historical, social (i.e., political, economic and technological), and vital situations.
5) A Catholic theological mediation in African American perspective must take note of the presence of Jesus of Nazareth at the center of the earliest African American religious discourse. It must grasp the demand for the concrete ongoing historicization of the vocation of Jesus, of his dynamic and saving message.
6) A Catholic theological mediation in African American perspective will prize interdisciplinarity. Adequate apprehension and understanding of the dense differentiated layers of the African, African American, Catholic *religious experience(s)* will require the collaborative work of theologians with biblical exegetes, anthropologists, geographers, linguists, ethnologists, musicologists, historians, art historians, historians of religions, cultural critics, literary critics, metaphysicians, ontologists, and philosophers.
7) African American theology will hold itself answerable to the threefold criteria of orthodoxy, orthopraxy, and orthopathy that not only meet the normative canons of truth, but nourish the moral and existential, the social and historical, the personal and interpersonal, the affective and psychic.

The ten Black bishops in their pastoral letter, *What We Have Seen and Heard,* note that Black leaders in the church—clergy, religious and lay—need encouragement and the authorization to use their competencies and to develop their expertise. They point out that the major hindrance to the full development of Black leadership within the church is still the fact of racism. They urge that on all levels the Catholic Church in the United States examine its conscience regarding its attitude toward Blacks, Hispanics, Native Americans and Asians. Blacks and other minorities still remain absent from many aspects of Catholic life and are only meagerly represented on the decision-making level. Some progress has been made in this regard, but there is still a long road ahead. Racism is surely a scandal but working to overcome it presents an important possibility for the renewal of the church.

Chapter Eight

Devotional Catholicism

The Encyclopedia of Catholicism defines "devotions" as: "Nonliturgical prayer forms that promote affective (and sometimes individualistic) attitudes of faith. They may also suggest a more effective response to personal religious needs than liturgical prayer."[1] *The New Dictionary of Theology* begins its treatment of devotions with the brief statement: "Devotions are the feeling side of Christian faith."[2] It is difficult to provide a concise definition of devotions since the devotional life encompasses a wide variety of practices and traditions. Some of the more popular Catholic devotions are the Rosary, Pilgrimages, Novenas, Adoration of the Blessed Sacrament, the Stations of the Cross, the Veneration of Saints, Marian devotions, and a host of others.

From the beginning of the history of the United States in 1776 until the decade of the 1840s there was little devotional life among Roman Catholics as a consequence of the Enlightenment and the Age of Reason. Statues and pictures found in Catholic churches in Europe were notably absent. With the flood of new immigrants in the decade of the 1840s the number of devotions increased dramatically. This cultivation of popular devotions as a distinct form of prayer has its origins in the Counter-Reformation as a response to the spiritual needs of Catholics who did not understand or feel fully at home in the Church's increasingly elaborate and complex liturgical celebrations. (Here liturgy refers to the official public worship of the Church: the Mass). Though Mass was celebrated in Latin, the language of the popular devotions was the vernacular which allowed the people the opportunity to pray in their mother tongue. The use of private devotions was revived by Pope Pius IX (1846–1878). In the United States devotional practices had already begun in the 1820s and with the continual arrival of millions of Catholic immigrants from Europe the number of devotions increased dramatically after 1840. The

Catholic bishops who were faced with the problem of ministering to these immigrants strongly encouraged the devotional life of the parishes as one way of helping the new arrivals maintain contact with their faith. By the 1860s devotional Catholicism had become a distinctive feature of the Church in this country.

The new immigrants brought their attachment to devotional Catholicism with them. The churches they built reflected this. They had many statues of saints, of the Sacred Heart of Jesus, of Mary, St. Joseph, St. Anthony, St. Patrick, and others. Stained glass windows, notably absent earlier, were imported from Europe. Religious festivals were another feature of devotional Catholicism. The crowning moment of the festival was the procession through the streets of the neighborhood. As Jay P. Dolan notes, by way of example:

> In East Harlem, New York City, Italians devoted an entire week in July to honor Our Lady of Mt. Carmel, a devotion imported from Italy. Even the statue of the Madonna of Mt. Carmel that had a place of honor in the church was brought from the old country.[3]

In Chicago, St. Louis, San Francisco, and in other cities Italian communities celebrated similar festivals in honor of the saints of the old country.[4] Other nationality groups had similar events.

Confraternities which were devotional increased dramatically in the 19th century. Among women the most popular confraternities were those honoring Mary, whereas for men one of the most popular confraternities was the Society of St. Vincent de Paul, which worked on behalf of the poor. Popular appeal of devotional Catholicism was aided in the late 19th century by the expansion of the print media. Magazines and newspapers promoted devotion to the saints. Devotion to Our Lady of Lourdes became very popular stemming from visions reported by a young peasant girl in 1858 at a grotto near the town of Lourdes in Southern France. As Jay P. Dolan remarks, "Devotion to Our Lady of Lourdes and the use of water collected at the shrine clearly underscored the European dimension to devotional Catholicism at this time."[5]

From 1920 until 1950 devotional Catholicism reached its highpoint. During this period Catholic piety was focused especially on Mass and the sacraments and on devotion to Mary. Mass attendance on Sunday was faithfully observed as was the reception of the sacraments. Marian devotions, which were very popular, included the recitation of the rosary, Marian feast days, May crownings of Marian statues, and the Mother of Sorrows novena. The apparition of Mary at Fatima, Portugal, in 1917 and the papal definition of her assumption into heaven by Pope Pius XII in 1950 further encouraged devotion to Mary.

Among the other popular devotions of this period, especially prior to Vatican II, were the Stations of the Cross, Benediction (now called Eucharistic Devotion), various novenas (prayers with a specific intention, offered on nine consecutive days), the Nine First Fridays (Mass and Communion on the first Fridays of nine consecutive months), and Forty Hours (adoration, procession, and benediction of the Blessed Sacrament to commemorate the 40 hours Jesus was in the tomb).

A major challenge to devotional Catholicism came from the liturgical movement in the 1940s and 1950s. By emphasizing the role of the laity and their participation in the church and at Mass, individual devotions so central to devotional Catholicism were being implicitly pushed aside. The 1950s were a boom time for religion in America. Church attendance attained record levels. The number of Catholics doubled between 1940 and 1960. By 1960 Roman Catholics numbered 40 million, approximately one-fourth of the entire population. The period of the immigrant church was coming to an end, but the religious culture for most Roman Catholics was still unchanged. But change was on the way.

In the earlier years of the decade of the 1950s the Catholic Church was thriving. It was the old immigrant Church at the peak of its influence. As Alan Ehrenhalt observes: "It was not searching for new identity. It was simply not interested in change. It cared about tradition and authority."[6] But as the decade continued the call for reform of the Church grew louder. Catholics had now become wealthier and better educated than their parents. Their move to the suburbs signaled the beginning of the end of the immigrant church. And with the election of Pope John XXIII in 1958 and his call for an ecumenical council, it seemed that change was going to take place. And as Jay P. Dolan writes:

> However, even if Vatican II had never happened, the renewal of Catholicism would still have taken place in the United States. That is because the social and cultural transformation of the post-World War II era proved to be as important if not indeed more important for American Catholics than Vatican II. Catholicism was indeed ripe for change, and change it would in a manner that would have been totally unexpected in 1960.[7]

Vatican II ushered in a new era of worship in the church. Modern languages replaced the use of Latin and the laity were encouraged to participate in the liturgy. The council also encouraged the adaptation of the Mass to the needs of different cultures. The uniformity of the Latin Mass was abandoned. The Mass was stressed as the summit and source of the Christian life and seen as the center of one's prayer life. As a result devotions such as the rosary, novenas in honor of the saints, benediction of the Blessed Sacrament, Forty Hours, and Stations of the Cross were pushed aside. The use of English at Mass undermined the uniqueness of English-language devotions and weakened their popularity. In their place Catholics have been encouraged to participate in a variety of social justice issues such as the civil rights movement, the war against poverty, working with the homeless, supporting ecological initiatives, and a variety of other causes. They have also been encouraged to participate in small Bible Study groups and in prayer groups. For many, such involvement replaced participation in traditional devotional practices.

In recent years, however, there has been a resurgence of traditional devotional practices. New devotions such as Bible Studies were not very successful for many. The disappearance of devotions created a spiritual void in the lives of many Catholics. There is no doubt that devotions are an important part of an individual's religion. As Michael S. Driscoll writes:

> In fact, to the extent that devotions can emerge with new religious symbols and reinterpret old ones, they will be meaningful and authentic. In their proper context and good use, devotions can be a means of connecting the past with the present in order to face the future. The necessity still remains of forging authentic devotional forms which will be expressive of contemporary and inculturated religious identity. Within American society, the search for identity continues. If devotions can be forged that will speak to people of a new generation, then they will reflect the genius of the American culture and further the mission of the American church.[8]

In the meantime, it seems clear, traditional devotions will remain an option for many Catholics, young and old alike. An interesting and informative analysis of these devotions is found in the recently published book *Awake My Soul: Contemporary Catholics on Traditional Devotions* edited by James Martin, S.J.[9]

It is important to note that the Second Vatican Council teaches that while devotions should be "warmly commended" and possess a "special dignity," they nevertheless remain subordinate to the Mass, which by its very nature far surpasses any of them."[10] A comprehensive guide published by the Vatican in 2001 makes clear that "the Liturgy and popular piety are two forms of worship which are in mutual and fruitful relationship with each other."[11] In other words, there is no conflict between loving the Mass on the one hand and having a devotion to Our Lady of Guadalupe on the other hand. The document goes on to express the hope that "other forms of piety among the Christian people are not overlooked, nor their useful contribution to living in unity with Christ, in the Church, be forgotten."[12] The writers who contributed essays to *Awake My Soul* deal with the following devotions: the Sacred Heart of Jesus, adoration of the Blessed Sacrament, pilgrimages, the saints, the Angelus, litanies, the Miraculous Medal, novenas, the Rosary, holy water, Our Lady of Guadalupe, First Fridays, *lectio divina*, the Immaculate Heart, relics, the Liturgy of the Hours, Mary, Joseph, and the stations of the cross. This list of devotions is not meant to be exhaustive. Rather, the essays try to explain some devotions "that may be ripe for a kind of renewal, or that have fallen into desuetude, or that may be less well known or understood by contemporary Catholics."[13] The brief essays can be very useful in rekindling one's devotional life.

Chapter Nine

The Charismatic Movement

(Renewal)

The charismatic movement has reminded Catholics of the role of the Holy Spirit in the life of the Church. Previous to the inception of the charismatic renewal in the 1960s, the Holy Spirit was not stressed in Catholic thinking in the same manner as it is today. And yet the Holy Spirit is the Paraclete (helper) promised by Jesus who will be with the Church until the Second Coming (see John 14:26). In the New Testament we learn how vital the Holy Spirit is to the life of the Christian community. We read of the transformation of the disciples by the reception of the Spirit at Pentecost, which marks the birth of the Church (Acts 2:3ff.). The presence of the Spirit manifests itself externally in such phenomena as the gifts of tongues and prophecy (I Cor. 12–15) and directs the officers of the Church in important decisions (Acts 13:2, 15:28, and 20:28). The list of the power of the Holy Spirit goes on and on as we read the pages of the New Testament.

Perhaps most important for the Church of today as well as for the Church of the future is the reminder the entire community receives from charismatic Catholics of the dynamic role of the Holy Spirit in the life of the Church. Those participating in the charismatic renewal lift up the teaching that the Holy Spirit is not restricted to those who belong to the charismatic renewal but rather is given to the entire Christian community. If there is to be an overall renewal of the Church, it will only be accomplished—all else not withstanding—through prayer and the power of the Holy Spirit. Surely it was by the power of the Holy Spirit that Vatican II was convened and brought to such a successful conclusion. The council explicitly teaches that it is the Holy Spirit who renews the Church. In *The Dogmatic Constitution on the Church* we read, "By the power of the Gospel He [the Holy Spirit] makes the Church grow, *perfectly renews her*, and leads her to perfect union with her Spouse [emphasis mine]."[1] And yet the charismatic renewal, despite its contributions,

has confused and, at times, angered those who are not involved in this seem-
ingly new episode in the history of the Church.

It is obvious that many American Catholics are, in fact, greatly disturbed
by the charismatic renewal that has been occurring in the Church since the
conclusion of Vatican II. Even though many of those same Catholics have no
significant firsthand experience of either Catholic charismatics or Protestant
pentecostals, they associate the two groups with one another and feel that the
"holy rollers" they heard so much about in their youth really have no place
within Catholicism. After all, such people seem to be fanatics, and their religion is fundamentalist, anti-intellectual, and anti-institutional. Their fundamentalism makes them intellectually inflexible and dogmatic in all their attitudes to the point where they confuse piety and theology. Such a pattern
makes them morally rigoristic. Further, they "speak in tongues," which to an
outsider appears to be nothing more than irrational babbling. They stress
Spirit-baptism and the experience of the Holy Spirit. If religion is based primarily on experience, aren't they on a collision course with their membership
in a structured church? And the objections go on. Yet the Catholic charismatic
renewal has not clashed with the hierarchy. As a matter of fact, the charismatic movement operates within the Church and with the blessing of the
American bishops. We will analyze the renewal to see why this is so, and we
will also try to clarify some of the misconceptions those outside the movement still hold. But at the outset it should be made clear that there are many
forms of piety within the Church that Catholics are free to accept or reject depending upon their own dispositions. The charismatic renewal is one example.

In the United States the charismatic renewal began at Duquesne University,
Pittsburgh, in 1963. It was not accidental that this occurred during the early
months of Vatican II. The council itself in *The Decree on the Ministry and
Life of Priests* put "renewal of the Church" in first place among the "three
pastoral goals of the Council," which it lists as "inner renewal of the Church,
the spread of the Gospel throughout the world, and dialogue with the modern
world."[2] And, as we have seen, the council teaches that it is the Holy Spirit
who renews the Church. The council also teaches that the role of the Holy
Spirit is to act as the giver of those gifts of the Spirit that lead to the renewal
of the Church. *The Dogmatic Constitution on the Church* states, "By these
gifts he [the Holy Spirit] makes them fit and ready to undertake the various
tasks or offices advantageous for the renewal and upbuilding of the Church."[3]
Many believe that this statement, among others, provided the theological
foundation of a "charismatic renewal of the Church."[4]

There was debate at the council concerning the gifts or charisms of the
Holy Spirit. Cardinal Ruffini argued that charisms have no important part to

play in the life of the modern Church even though they were greatly in evidence in the apostolic era. He went on to say that such gifts (e.g., speaking in tongues and healing) subsequently became so rare as to have practically ceased. Cardinal Suenens' reply to Ruffini, which prevailed at the council, maintained that the charisms are not "peripheral or accidental phenomenon in the life of the Church, but rather are of vital importance for the building up of the mystical body."[5]

A logical question would then be, "How would such charisma manifest themselves in the concrete?" To answer this question it is first necessary to define what is meant by a charism. A charism is a manifestation of the Holy Spirit (1 Cor. 12:7), a coming to visibility of the Spirit who operates in each person for the common good (1 Cor. 12:6), that is, in the service of the Church and the world. Such charisms or gifts are many and are given by the Spirit at will. All Christians have such gifts, but they must be utilized if reform is to be effective. Indeed St. Paul taught that the Holy Spirit "distributes different gifts to different people just as he chooses" (1 Cor. 12:11). *The Dogmatic Constitution on the Church* states, "These charismatic gifts whether they be the most outstanding or the more simple and widely diffused, are to be received with thanksgiving and consolation, for they are exceedingly suitable and useful for the needs of the Church."[6] Such charisms manifest themselves in the concrete in every Catholic parish throughout the world. Parishioners would have a role and a ministry according to the gifts they had received from the spirit for the upbuilding of the community. And at the parish level each person would have the opportunity to use the gifts he or she had received under the leadership of their pastor. In a real sense, then, all Catholics are charismatic, and all are called to share their gifts with the entire Christian community.

But what of those who belong to the charismatic renewal in the narrower sense, namely, those who attend prayer meetings and are involved with Spirit-baptism, speaking in tongues, healing, and prophecy? These people tend to pray with their hands upraised and their eyes closed! Aren't they rather elitist in their attitude and perhaps even pharisaical? There is no easy answer to this question because some charismatics may well fit this description. But this would refer only to a small fringe of the renewal. Charismatics know that to concentrate only on the more extraordinary gifts of the Holy Spirit, or to claim to be superior Christians, is unacceptable.

Though the term *movement* is being used in reference to the charismatic renewal, it should be pointed out that the adherents of the renewal try to avoid this word since it carries some negative connotations. The term is borrowed from cultural anthropology and in many ways can be correctly applied to the renewal.[7] At the popular level, however, a kind of distortion often takes place by putting the term into a theological context. From this perspective, charismatic movement is used to refer to a kind of capturing of the Holy Spirit and his gifts by the members of the movement. Often those using the term in this narrower sense restrict the meaning of charism to the "word gifts" such as tongues, prophecy, interpretation, wisdom, and knowledge. Lest any such limiting connotation be placed on them, large numbers of Catholic charismatics no longer use the term *Catholic charismatic movement* and have instead adopted the term *Catholic charismatic renewal*. They have done so because those within the renewal do not claim to be the only ones who possess the Holy Spirit and the charisms. They know that these gifts belong to the entire Christian community. What they desire and pray will happen is that all members of the Church will open themselves up to the full spectrum of gifts that are offered by the Holy Spirit.

The Catholic charismatic renewal, as indicated earlier, began at Duquesne University in Pittsburgh in 1963 and soon took root at the University of Notre Dame and the University of Michigan as well. The renewal quickly spread, and by 1970 there were many prayer groups scattered throughout the United States. Spontaneous prayer meetings had been going on for several years before 1966 at both Duquesne and Notre Dame but now became infused with charismatic elements. Though certain parallels can be found in the Wesleyan-Holiness tradition, the Catholic renewal drew heavily from contemporary Catholic spirituality. For example, many of the earliest members had belonged to the Cursillo movement that long had practiced small group spontaneous prayers as well as group reunions where participants spoke freely to one another of their experiences of Christ. So when the first group of Catholics from Duquesne, who were curious about and very interested in the phenomenon referred to as "baptism in the Holy Spirit," attended a neo-Pentecostal prayer meeting conducted by Methodists, Episcopalians, Presbyterians, and some members of denominational Pentecostal churches, they felt fairly comfortable. The meeting took place while sitting in a circle in a living room. The Catholics found the structure and many of the elements of the service rather similar to their own practice of group prayer. They soon started their own prayer meetings and structured it in a similar manner.

Most Catholic prayer groups have as few as ten and as many as one hundred participants. Prayer meetings, which form the core of the renewal, are usually held once a week, though this varies. They are often structured so that all sit in a circle facing one another. As groups become larger, seating is arranged in concentric circles. This arrangement encourages each member to share his or her particular gifts with the whole community. The emphasis is on the presence of Christ in the midst of his people. Stress is also placed on the priesthood of all the faithful and on the diversity of ministries to be found within the Church.

Generally a prayer meeting begins with the singing of hymns, although music is interspersed throughout the service. Handclapping and rhythmic bodily swaying often accompany the congregational singing. The leader of the meeting then welcomes everyone and encourages them to participate in faith and to focus their hearts on the Lord's presence in their midst. He or she also encourages all to use their spiritual gifts properly. The use of gifts occurs throughout the meeting. Spontaneous prayer regularly includes the use of tongues, prophecy, and testimony. Many groups choose a speaker to give testimony, teach, or preach. Following this, a few minutes of common silence is observed. Toward the end of the meeting members often express their personal intentions, needs, and requests for prayer.

In contrast to the Pentecostal order of service, Catholic prayer meetings usually do not end with an "altar call" or an invitation for those who do not belong to the group to ask for baptism in the Spirit at their initial meeting. Rather the meeting is directed toward worship in praise and thanksgiving to God the Almighty Father through Jesus as Lord and Savior that is carried out through the power of the Holy Spirit. Preparation for initiation into a Catholic charismatic prayer group occurs for the most part by means of a program that is called the "Life in the Spirit Seminar,"[8] which was developed by the Word of God, a charismatic community in Ann Arbor, Mich. The seminar removes the event of Spirit-baptism from the realm of an isolated religious experience and places it in the context of a basic explanation of the Gospel, of conversion to Jesus, and of the need for the power to the Holy Spirit to live a full Christian life. The event of Spirit-baptism is placed at the center of the ongoing need of a mature Christian life of prayer, study, service, and involvement in the Christian community. The "Life in the Spirit Seminar" is made up of seven instructions that are given by the leader of the seminar team. He or she is aided by several men and women from the prayer group who serve as team members. Small discussion groups are formed, and all pray that the newcomers may commit or recommit their lives to Christ and accept the workings of the Holy Spirit in their lives.

Praying for baptism in the Spirit takes place during the fifth session of the seminars. The session opens with some preliminary remarks from the leader who explains that the group will make a commitment to Christ and that there will be prayers of exorcism and the laying on of hands. Then, after an opening hymn and a period of prayer, those who are praying over the candidates exorcise each of them and lay hands on them, praying for them to be baptized in the Spirit. Exorcism here refers to casting out evil spirits or telling evil spirits to leave a person or place. It does not imply that a person is possessed by evil spirits. When everyone is finished praying, the leader calls the whole group together. By this time some of the newcomers have usually received the gift of tongues, and those who have not are asked to pray for this gift. Everyone who has completed the seminar is asked to remain in the prayer group and to continue the process that has begun by joining one of the growth courses or Bible studies offered by the group.

Spirit-baptism, which is such an important concept in the renewal, refers to a group of Christians praying over one of its members so that he or she will receive the Holy Spirit in its fullness, as did the apostles on Pentecost Sunday. The term also refers to the divine response to this prayer, especially as it affects the life of the person who is being "baptized." Some Pentecostal churches identify Spirit-baptism with the reception of the gift of tongues, no doubt because tongues (glossolalia) is a very fundamental charism. But this is not so in Catholicism. To make such an identification is seen to be presumptuous since it is up to the will of the Holy Spirit to deal with each person according to that individual's specific spiritual needs. Catholic charismatics simply disagree with those who demand the gift of tongues as the only certain proof of the presence of the Spirit or who regard the gift as an absolute precondition for authentic possession of the other charismatic gifts.

Some Catholics are afraid that those in the charismatic renewal may be practicing a fraudulent version of the sacrament of confirmation. But this is not the case. Spirit-baptism is not understood to be a sacrament. The group that prays with an individual gathers around that person not to administer a sacrament but because they wish to express, by an external sign—namely, the laying on of hands—that they are joining their prayers to those of the person who is seeking a fuller share in the gifts of the Holy Spirit. Baptism and confirmation are sacraments of initiation into the living of the Christian life and can be received only once, although it is believed that the special graces of each sacrament are present throughout one's life. And so it is deemed appropriate that a confirmed Christian turn to God to beg for greater docility to the grace of confirmation, and that his or her prayer should be supported by other members of the Christian community. Those who thus join their prayers with those of the person in question are expressing their solidarity not only with the individual but also with the bishop who confirmed him or her. In Spirit-baptism individuals, in effect, are asking the Holy Spirit to take them in their present state of spiritual development and to transform them. Spirit-baptism is basically a prayer to the Father in the name of Jesus that the Holy Spirit will come upon a person who has decided to break with sin and seek the light of Christ. It is a form of prayer that seeks the individual to be fully docile to the inspirations of the Holy Spirit and completely open to whatever charismatic gifts the Holy Spirit may offer. In terms of its effects it is commonly observable that those who receive Spirit-baptism have an experience with the triune God that produces a new or greater desire for prayer and a stronger desire to know the Scriptures. There is also a deeper awareness of God's presence as well as an increase of love together with a greater ability to express that love.

What most intrigues many people about the charismatic renewal is the gift of speaking in tongues. Most charismatics deplore the excessive emphasis on glossolalia in discussions about their movement. Yet this phenomenon inevitably attracts attention because it is so unusual and spectacular in nature. Many outsiders consider it bizarre and irritating and, most of all, unnecessary for the practice of Christian living, although it is very commonly practiced among Pentecostal and charismatic Christians. Why is this done and what does it mean? Before processing further it might prove helpful to note that many great movements of spiritual renewal through the years have often emphasized notions that seemed to be unusual and even bizarre such as the gift of tears, fasting, the breathing techniques of hesychasm, and the yoga and zen postures of meditation. These practices, however, serve as catalysts for opening spiritual paths that have been blocked by inhibitions and barriers that are often erected by various peoples and that stand in the way of a vital relationship with God.

The word *glossolalia* comes from two Greek words: *glossa*, which means "tongues" and *lalein*, which means "to speak." The verb *lalein* can signify any utterance of sound whether it be intelligent or intelligible. *Glossa* can mean "language" in the broadest sense such as that used by whales or elephants, for example. It can also refer to a specific language in the narrower sense, such as English or French, in which specific words and grammar are used. In reference to the gift of glossolalia, it can be used collectively by a whole group or by an individual. When an individual speaks in tongues it is not mumbling or gibberish. Rather as René Laurentin observes, the speaker "utters a rhythmic sequence of distinct, articulated, structured sounds (or syllables) that possess a degree of coherence and phonetic clarity."[9]

When a person speaks in tongues he or she is not delirious or in a trance. The speaker remains in full possession of his or her senses, but what is said is usually not understood by the person speaking or the people who are present. The speaker is aware of what he or she is doing and of what is happening outside the experience and can cease speaking in tongues at any point. Someone in the group inevitably is given the gift of interpretation of tongues, which refers to an intuitive understanding of the meaning. Interpretation does not refer to a translation of what has been articulated.

But why speak in tongues at all? Why not simply speak in a rational and, even, spontaneous manner when addressing God? Does not the use of glossolalia put

religion in a bad light and hold it up to the ridicule and disdain of many believers and nonbelievers alike? To answer these questions it is necessary to point out
that glossolalia is a very specific mode of prayer. Those who speak in tongues
agree that to do so has a liberating effect. It removes many inhibitions and di-
minishes the fear of approaching the ineffable God. It aids one to pray more frequently and to become more aware both of one's own sinfulness and of God's
greatness. It strengthens intercessory prayer, which is often inhibited, as St. Paul
tells us in Rom. 8:26 by the fact that "we cannot choose words in order to pray
properly." Glossolalia is a kind of sacred language. To speak in tongues is also
to use a kind of sacred language for prayer. Until recently this role was played
by the use of Latin during Catholic Mass, which was a kind of sacred language
set over ordinary language. The fact that so many Catholics greatly miss the use
of Latin helps explain that it is not by chance that the use of glossolalia appeared
within Catholicism at about the same time that Latin disappeared. Glossolalia,
then, is a preconceptual, nonrational language by which one speaks to God as the
Wholly Other.

Glossolia, like the other gifts of the Holy Spirit, is given to render Christians more docile to the spirit of Christ so that the recipients might become
more like Christ, the Spirit-filled Messiah. It is a gift of prayer and, in its use,
as is true of all the gifts, it must be regulated by the law of Christ-like love as
St. Paul reminds us in 1 Cor. 12–14.

Some would still agree with St. Augustine who wrote that certain charismatic gifts, among them the gift of tongues, were given by the Holy Spirit to
the apostolic community to help enable the establishment of the Church. Augustine went on to argue that once the Church was formed into a cohesive
whole, these gifts were withdrawn and replaced by other gifts. This is a de-
fensible thesis, but it cannot conclusively be proven or disproven.[10] What is
certain, however, is that this theory is but one hypothesis among many in reference to the purpose of the charismatic gifts. It is surely not a dogma of the
Church. And since the Holy Spirit is free to grant his gifts any time and any
place, it is presumptuous to think that he is limited by the theological utter-
ances of even one as great as St. Augustine, or by any other theologian.

There are several dangers inherent in the Catholic charismatic renewal.

1. There is the danger of *separation*, that is, of leaving communion with
   Rome and establishing an independent community, as has been evidenced
   at times. Yet the charismatic movement generally has been marked by a
   firm attachment to the Church and its leadership. There simply has been
   no confrontation of any significance against church hierarchy. To avoid
   such problems, prayer groups within the United States rarely celebrate
   Mass at their meetings in order not to entice members away from their
   parish Masses. To avoid competition with the Sunday services in their

parishes, charismatics normally avoid having their weekly meetings on a Saturday or Sunday.

2. There is the danger of *fundamentalism*, that is, the naively literal and "obvious" interpretation of Scripture. Such an attitude ties the spirit to the letter of the Bible. Surely some Catholic charismatics are fundamentalist in this sense. But they are a distinct minority, and when they do dominate it usually indicates a manifestation of poor leadership in the group. On the whole, the movement is quite open to contemporary exegesis. At the same time, Catholic charismatics do practice a straightforward reading of the Bible that emphasizes the spiritual nourishment that can be gained by so doing. But, generally speaking, they are no more fundamentalists than other Catholics, and usually are far more devoted to reading and listening to the Word of God.

3. A third danger is that of *emotionalism*, meaning that charismatics tend to focus on feeling at the expense of reason. It is certainly true that the movement values the emotive level and encourages the expression of feelings. In doing so, there can be an overemphasis on the emotions. Basically, however, this movement recognizes that we must love God with our whole person, which includes not only the intellect and will, but the emotions as well. Everyone is different, and some people are very unemotional. But obviously many people join this movement, at least in part, because they do feel a need to express their emotions as they worship Christ, who is the "Lord of the Dance." This aspect of the charismatic movement should not be seen as a liability, but as an achievement.

4. A fourth danger, and one that brings the most frequent and serious criticism of the charismatic movement, is that it is *too introverted* and, thus, turns its membership away from involvement in areas of social justice. The complaint is that charismatics focus on individual relationships but not on their responsibilities to society. This complaint was far more common in the late 1960s and early 1970s during the era of the Vietnam War. And it had a basis in circumstance. But as the charismatic movement has matured, so has the involvement of many prayer groups in areas of social concern. Today it would be fair to say that those in the charismatic movement are involved in areas of social justice in at least as great a measure as is true of the Christian population in general. This, however, is not to discount the fact that there seems to be an overall lack of participation at the political level and the level of social justice by Christians in the United States.

Much remains to be discussed concerning the Catholic charismatic renewal such as detailed explanations of the meaning of *healing, prophecy,* and other gifts. It can be said that the charismatic renewal is serving as a remedy for many who had been suffering from spiritual aridity. Charismatic communities are not only dynamic vehicles for prayer, but they also provide an outlet for likeminded Christians who are attempting to develop deeper relationships with Christ. This emphasis on community is an important element in the charismatic renewal and is necessary for the reinvigorating of the Church as a whole. The charismatic renewal is also rediscovering the Gospel as the "good news" and as a source of rejuvenation for true Christian living. The movement continues to profit from the enthusiasm that characterizes all beginnings. The scope and historical importance of the movement will be determined by the test of time. It already seems evident that in the coming years only a relatively small percentage of American Catholics will be members of the charismatic renewal. But the importance of the movement, both now and in the future, will remain essentially constant. Charismatic Catholics will continue to serve as an important reminder to the Catholic population as a whole that the continual renewal of the Church is the work of the Holy Spirit, and that the gifts of the Holy Spirit, in some fashion, are given to all Christians. Since all are called to the perfection of holiness, all will be expected to share their gifts with the Christian community for the continual upbuilding of the Body of Christ.

SUMMARY

The charismatic renewal began in the United States in the mid-1960s. Perhaps most important for the Church of today as well as for the Church of the future is the reminder the entire Christian community receives from charismatic Catholics of the dynamic role of the Holy Spirit in the life of the Church, and that the Holy Spirit is not restricted to those who belong to the charismatic renewal, but is given to the entire Christian community. A further reminder is provided by charismatic Catholics that all Christians are called to a life of prayer and devotion to the sacred Scriptures. If there is to be an overall renewal of the Church, it will only be accomplished, all else not withstanding, by Christians who continually open themselves to the power of the Holy Spirit.

Many Catholics are disturbed by the charismatic renewal and feel that those who belong to the movement are "holy rollers." Yet the renewal operates within the Church and with the blessing of the American bishops. There are safeguards in relation to the gifts of the Spirit, such as speaking in tongues and healing, that must be observed. To this end "Life in the Spirit Seminars" are conducted to provide proper theological and spiritual direction.

When noncharismatics hear the term *Spirit-baptism* they are often afraid that those in the charismatic renewal may be practicing a fraudulent version of the sacrament of confirmation. But this is not the case. Spirit-baptism is not understood to be a sacrament. The group that prays with an individual for Spirit-baptism gathers around that person not to administer a sacrament but to express, by an external sign, namely, the laying on of hands, that they are joining their prayers to those of the person who is seeking a fuller share in the gifts of the Holy Spirit. In terms of its effect, it is commonly observable that those who receive Spirit-baptism have an experience of the triune God that produces a new or greater desire for prayer and a stronger desire to know the Scriptures.

The gift of speaking in tongues (glossolalia) offends many noncharismatics. But to speak in tongues is to use a kind of sacred language for prayer. Glossolalia, like the other gifts of the Holy Spirit, is given to render Christians more docile to the Spirit of Christ so that the recipients might become more like Christ, the Spirit-filled Messiah. It is a gift of prayer and its use, as is true of all the gifts, must be regulated by the law of Christ-like love as St. Paul reminds us in 1 Cor. 12–14. Yet there are dangers inherent in the use of these gifts that must be controlled through solid theological teaching, as St. Paul admonishes.

Chapter Ten

"Spiritual" but Not "Religious"

The United States is perhaps the most religious nation on earth. Opinion polls indicate that over 90 percent of all Americans believe in some kind of higher power. Sixty-two percent belong to a church, synagogue, mosque or temple. Approximately 38 percent of Americans are not affiliated with organized religion but claim to be strongly spiritual.

Robert C. Fuller in his excellent study *Spiritual but Not Religious: Understanding Unchurched America*, distinguishes three types of unchurched Americans.[1] He begins by stating that the unchurched aren't all alike.

The first group he discusses isn't religious at all. In fact he believes that somewhere between 8 and 15 percent of the total population can be considered wholly nonreligious. They consider themselves neither religious nor spiritual. He notes that Wade Clark Roof's studies of the Baby Boomer generation indicates that 15 percent of the Boomers are secularist, simply not interested in religion or spirituality.[2] In other words, approximately one in seven Americans are completely indifferent to religion and spirituality.

A second group of unchurched Americans in Fuller's overview have an ambiguous relationship with organized religion. In this group are those who belong to a church but rarely attend as well as those who often attend church but choose not to be formally affiliated. It is indeed possible that some of these persons are quite spiritual. About 10 percent of the population have such ambiguous relationships to organized religion and perhaps half of these could be placed in the third group.

The third group of unchurched individuals should be considered religious in some sense. This is the largest group of the unchurched and includes as many as 21 percent of the entire American population. These are people who are truly concerned with spirituality and spiritual issues. Many of them find religious institutions stifling. There is a separation for them between the realm of religious experience and the public realm of formal religious practice. This group can clearly be referred to as "spiritual but not religious."

The words "spiritual" and "religious" are really synonyms. Before the 20th century the words were used more or less interchangeably. However, as Fuller observes:

> The word *spiritual* gradually came to be associated with the private realm of thought and experience while the word *religious* came to be connected with the public realm of membership in religious institutions, participation in formal rituals, and adherence to official denominational doctrines.[3]

Fuller writes that a group of social scientists studied 346 people who represented a wide range of religious backgrounds in an attempt to clarify what is implied when individuals describe themselves as "spiritual but not religious." They found that religiousness was associated with regular church attendance and acceptance of orthodox beliefs, whereas spirituality was associated with higher levels of interest in mysticism, experimentation with unorthodox beliefs and practices, and negative feelings toward both clergy and churches.[4] Those who describe themselves as "spiritual, but not religious" reject organized religion as the only, or even the most valuable, means of developing their spirituality. Instead they practice an individualized spirituality which includes choosing from a wide variety of religious teachings. These individuals are more likely to have a college education, to be liberal in their political views, to have parents who do not attend church frequently, and to be more independent in the sense of having weaker social relationships.[5]

Many Americans, including a disproportionately high percentage of those who attended college in the 1960s and 1970s, blamed Western religions for their complicity in producing our excessive materialistic culture. They wanted a spirituality that would free them from their cultural conditioning and would help prepare them for an ecstatic experience of "cosmic consciousness." Many were drawn to Eastern religions such as Buddhism and Hinduism. Or they studied and practiced Transcendental Meditation. In the recent past, as a matter of fact, Americans have been exposed to nonbiblical religious ideas to an extent unprecedented in Western cultural history.

It is probably fair to say that 20 percent of the population in this country are sympathetic with New Age ideas, not counting members of churches who are somewhat influenced by these alternative approaches. The origins of the term "New Age" are not clear. And there is no clear definition of what designates an alternative spirituality as New Age. Many who are looking for new sources of spiritual understanding are attracted to New Age thinking. Those who follow such an approach are usually disengaged from existing churches and for them organized religion and the biblical heritage are "old age."

Fuller observes that few people who are "spiritual but not religious" believe that there is one, single truth that will address all of their intellectual and emotional needs. But most are sure of three things, namely:

> First, they believe it has come time for religions to abandon "old age" dogmatism and incorporate contemporary knowledge. For a religion to be viable in our era it must draw eclectically from science, modern psychology, and the best insights of all world religions. Second, religion must have practical applications in our everyday lives. It must be more psychological than theological. That is, it should be primarily concerned with helping us to find fulfillment in the here and now of this life (rather than devoting most of its attention to some speculative afterlife). And, third, metaphysical seekers yearn for an experiential spirituality; they are bored with what they perceive to be the lifeless rituals of established churches and feel the need for some kind of mystical connection with God.[6]

The quest for spirituality among New Agers includes a wide variety of approaches which tend to be strongly gnostic, that is, they emphasize esoteric knowledge (enlightenment) in attaining salvation or integrity. Contemporary New Agers reflect the influence of Carl Jung who predicted an "Age of Aquarius" dominated by true science and world humanism which would succeed the present "Age of Pisces," the violent Christian era. An era of peace, love, and prosperity is anticipated following an interval of social chaos.

There is no such thing as an organized New Age movement. Those interested in one alternative spiritual approach may have no interest in other areas that are considered to be New Age. New Age religion extends to a wide range of interest in the supernatural including archaic, arcane and occult beliefs and practices of Asian, African, and other mythical, religious, philosophical, and magical traditions, such as karmic retribution, reincarnation, psychic powers, and nature lore, including paganism (witchcraft). Elements of Hinduism, Buddhism, Sufism, Cabalism, spiritualism ("channeling"), and numerology may also be present.

New Age religion also extends to astrology, Ouija boards, tarot cards, the *I Ching*, and even to the fantasy worlds of science fiction. Other characteristic concerns include planetary healing, holistic health, self-improvement, and the rights of women, minorities, and animals. Nonconventional health care includes acupuncture, biofeedback, herbal medicine, hypnosis, massage, organic gardening, vegetarianism, and other alternative therapies using crystals, colors, aromas, etc.

It is difficult to know how many Americans are sympathetic to New Age spirituality since very few people use the term when describing their own religious beliefs. But as was indicated earlier, it seems that about 20 percent of the American public are included in this category.

Interestingly, on the whole, psychology has had a special affinity with America's unchurched spiritual traditions. In fact unchurched spiritualities tend to utilize a psychological vocabulary. As Fuller remarks:

This vocabulary (1) highlights the spiritual dimensions of the unconscious mind and (2) suggests self-help strategies for living in creative harmony with God.[7]

Carl Jung, who died in 1961, was influential in connecting psychology with spiritual thought. He argued that in addition to the personal unconscious described by Sigmund Freud, human beings also have a point of inner connection with the "collective unconscious." This was Jung's way of referring to God in a psychological vocabulary befitting the modern era. Jung's psychology focused on what he called the individuation process, a lifelong path of self-discovery and self-transformation. His spiritually charged writings succeeded in making the concept of God (the collective unconscious) relevant to a class of educated persons, many of whom were repelled by traditional religious language. However, it was Reverend Normal Vincent Peale who converted many Americans to what can be called the gospel of the unconscious. Peale served a number of Methodist churches before becoming pastor of one of the most prestigious churches in America, the Marble Collegiate Church in New York City, a church which belonged to the conservative Dutch Reformed Church in America. Its members tended to be well-educated and wealthy and aware of cultural developments.

In 1952 Peale published *The Power of Positive Thinking* which was to become one of the most influential books in American religious history.[8] This book certainly did not deal with the Reformed theology of John Calvin but rather was aimed at how God could make a difference in one's spiritual life. He described God as a power available to individuals in their daily lives. He taught that by channeling spiritual power through your thoughts you can have peace of mind, improved health, and a never-ceasing flow of energy. In articulating this psychological gospel, Peale did not turn to the great theologians of the Protestant tradition. Rather he cited Ralph Waldo Emerson and William James to make a case for the Christian character of his teaching that our unconscious minds have continual access to the spiritual power that flows through the universe. For Peale, human desire, not God's grace, predominates and he was even less respectful of the notion of sin. His teaching had nothing to do with the need to seek forgiveness of sin. Rather he was concerned about correcting personality traits that prevent a person from connecting with the power of God. One of the first to notice this shift in thinking was the noted psychologist Karl Menninger who wrote *Whatever Became of Sin* in 1973.[9] Menninger's main thesis was that in unquestionably adopting psychological theories Christian ministers simultaneously strayed from their biblical foundations. This would include Dr. Peale. And as Roy Anker observes it is impossible to overestimate "the role that Peale and especially *The Power of Positive Thinking* played in inserting New Thought theology into the mainstream of American religion and thereby reshaping the core, mood, and configurations of American religious life."[10]

Robert Wuthnow's study of spirituality in America since the 1950s indicates that "a traditional spirituality of inhabiting sacred places has given way to a new spirituality of seeking."[11] In speaking of "habitation spirituality" he is referring to the spirituality associated with formal religious institutions. Habitation spirituality is what occurs in churches, synagogues, mosques and temples which includes formal worship, traditional creeds, and loyalty to a particular religious heritage. Such spirituality offers security, and stability to its members. On the other hand, seeker spirituality represents the spiritual style of a sojourner who foregoes the security of habitation spirituality in exchange for more personal freedom.

In the recent past bookstores such as Borders, Barnes & Noble and others have served as centers of unchurched spirituality. These stores have large sections entitled Christianity, Judaica, and Islam. Large sections are devoted to books on Eastern Religions, New Age Thought, and self help philosophies. The boundaries of American religion are clearly being redrawn. A good 20 percent of the American population consider themselves to be "spiritual but not religious." And this new eclecticism shapes the piety of many members of established religions.

Wade Clark Roof argues that "the cleavage between the so-called churched and unchurched sectors has widened for this generation."[12] In Europe this gap separates the relatively small number of those who are churched from the nonreligious majority. Only a small segment in the United States are totally secular and unconcerned about spirituality. The rest of the unchurched are, though in varying degrees, spiritual but not religious. In the United States the gap separating the churched and unchurched refers to how people are religious, not whether they are religious.

In the 1960s many social scientists predicted that the United States would follow Europe and steadily abandon church affiliation and become ever more secularized, but this has not occurred. Instead of secularization leading to the eradication of spiritual interests, societal changes have led many Americans to explore different approaches to the question of spirituality.

How do these recent developments affect Roman Catholicism? Certainly many are seeking a deeper spirituality and are asking for guidance in doing so. Many parishes are offering Bible studies, days of recollection, retreats, seminars, various devotions such as novenas, the Rosary, and during Lent, the

Stations of the Cross. Authors such as Thomas Merton, Henry Nouwen, Ronald Rolheiser, Anne Carr, Sandra Schneiders and others, past and present, have produced outstanding books on spirituality and spiritual guidance. It is up to the individual Catholic to make use of the treasury that has been offered and to make a commitment to deepening his/her spiritual life. To do so is not easy, but the rewards are surely worth the effort.

Conclusion

Many social scientists in the 1960s predicted that Americans would soon follow the European pattern and eventually abandon church affiliation in favor of secular attitudes. They argued that this was an inevitable process. But they were wrong. Even most of the unchurched haven't abandoned their spiritual interests. Certainly science, technology, increased social mobility and secularization have had a great impact. The practice of spirituality has changed, but not as dramatically for Roman Catholics as one might think. As was mentioned at the end of Chapter 8, the Church offers many possible approaches to a deeper prayer life and the development of one's spiritual life. There is indeed a treasury of spiritual approaches to draw from. It is up to the individual Catholic to make use of these gifts. As Christians it is important that we work to develop our inner spiritual lives. We should make time in our busy day to set time aside for prayer and meditation. We should attempt to create a solitude of heart as we deepen our relationship with Christ. In doing so we not only deepen our spirituality but achieve a peace, love and joy which the world cannot give.

Notes

CHAPTER 1. THE NEW RELIGIOUS AMERICA

1. Diana Eck, *The New Religious America* (New York: Harper Collins, 2001).

2. Will Herberg, *Protestant, Catholic, Jew* (Chicago: University of Chicago Press, 1983).

3. Ibid., 40

4. Ibid.

5. Eck, 70.

6. Austin Flannery, *Vatican Council II, The Conciliar and Post Conciliar Documents* (Northport, N.Y.: Costello Publishing Co., 1992), 461.

7. Robert Wuthnow, *After Heaven: Spirituality in America Since the 1950s* (Berkeley, Calif.: University of California Press, 1998), VIII.

8. Ibid., 2.

9. See Theodore Caplow et al., *Recent Social Trends in the United States, 1960–1999* (Montreal: McGill-Queens University Press, 1991), 289.

10. Wuthnow, 6.

11. See Gerald Strober and Ruth Tomczak, Jerry Falwell: *A Flame for God* (Nashville, Tenn.: Nelson, 1979).

12. Pat Robertson, *The Secret Kingdom* (Nashville, Tenn.: Nelson, 1982), 29.

13. Wuthnow, 110.

14. Ibid., 113.

15. Quoted in F. Lynne Bachleda, "Angels in America," *Publishers Weekly,* 12 July 1993), 31.

16. Joel S. Goldsmith, *The Art of Meditation* (San Francisco: Harper San Francisco, 1958), 27.

17. Alasdair MacIntyre, *After Virtue: A Study in Moral Theory*, 2nd ed. (Notre Dame, Ind.: University of Notre Dame Press, 1984), 194.

18. Jack Kornfield, *A Path with Heart: A Guide through the Perils and Promises of Spiritual Life* (New York: Bantam Books, 1993), 34.

19. Joan Chittister, *Wisdom Distilled from the Daily: Living the Rule of St. Benedict Today* (New York: Harper Collins, 1991), 35.

CHAPTER 2. SPIRITUALITY TODAY

1. Sandra Schneiders, "Theology and Spirituality: Strangers, Rivals, or Partners," in *The Catholic Faith: A Reader,* ed. Lawrence S. Cunningham (New York/Mahwah, N.J., Paulist Press, 1988), 241.
2. Ibid.
3. Flannery, 397.
4. Philip Murnion, "The Community Called Parish," in *The Catholic Faith: A Reader*, ed. Lawrence S. Cunningham, op. cit., 181.
5. Roland Rolheiser, *The Holy Longing: The Search for a Christian Spirituality* (New York: Doubleday, 1999), 11.
6. Ibid.
7. Ibid., 32.
8. Henri Nouwen, *Reaching Out: The Three Movements of the Spiritual Life* (New York: Doubleday, 1975).
9. Rolheiser, 53.
10. John Shea, *Stories of Faith* (Chicago: Thomas More Press, 1980).
11. Jerome Murphy O'Connor, *Becoming Human Together* (Wilmington, Del.: Michael Glazier Press, 1977), 202–203.
12. Andrew Greeley, *The Catholic Myth* (New York: Charles Scribner's Sons, 1990), 144–145.
13. Philip Murnion, "The Community Called Parish," in *The Catholic Faith: A Reader,* 183.
14. Ibid., 183–190.
15. Ibid., 188.
16. Rolheiser, 161.
17. Nouwen, 26.
18. Ibid., 41.
19. Anne Morrow Lindbergh, *Gift from the Sea* (New York: Pantheon Books, 1955), 40.
20. Thomas Merton, *The Sign of Jonas* (Garden City, N.Y.: Image Books, 1956), 261.
21. Nouwen, 79.
22. Ibid., 124.
23. Ibid., 125.

CHAPTER 3. CHRISTIAN MYSTICS AND SPIRITUAL WRITERS

1. Richard P. McBrien, *Catholicism* (San Francisco: Harper Collins, 1994), 1052.
2. Denys the Areopagite, *The Mystical Theology in the Complete Works of Pseudo-Dionysius* (London: C. Luibherd, 1987).

3. Clement of Alexandria, *Pedagogue (The Tutor)* (New York: Fathers of the Church, Inc., 1954), and *Stromateis (Miscellanies)* (New York: Fathers of the Church, Inc., 1953).

4. St. Augustine, *Confessions,* trans. by Henry Chadwick (Oxford: Oxford University Press, 1991).

5. St. Catherine of Siena, *The Dialogue.* Trans. with an introduction by Suzanne Noffke (New York: Paulist Press, 1980), 1.

6. Ibid., 167.

7. Ibid.

8. Ibid.

9. See Julian of Norwich, *Showings*, edited and trans. by Edmund Colledge and James Walsh (New York: Paulist Press, 1978).

10. Ibid., chap. 86.

11. Ibid., chap. 2.

12. Ibid., chap. 27.

13. Ibid., chap. 58.

14. Ignatius of Loyola, *Spiritual Exercises*, trans. by Louis J. Puke (Chicago: Loyola Press, 1951).

15. St. Teresa of Avila, *Life, The Way of Perfection, Foundations, The Interior Castle.* See *The Collected Works of St. Teresa of Avila*, trans. by Kiernan Kavanaugh (Washington, D.C.; ICS Publications, 1980).

16. *Life,* VIII, 5.

17. *The Way of Perfection,* (XXVI, 1–6).

18. St. John of the Cross, *The Ascent of Mt. Carmel* and *The Dark Night of the Soul.* See *The Collected Works of St. John of the Cross*, 2nd ed. trans. by Kiernan Kavanaugh and Otilio Rodriguez (Washington, D.C.: ICS Publications, 1979).

19. *The Dark Night of the Soul*, II, 24, ii.

20. St. Francis de Sales, *Introduction to the Devout Life* (Garden City, N.Y.: Image Books, 1955).

21. Edith Stein, *The Science of the Cross: A Study of St. John of the Cross*, trans. by Hilda Graef (Chicago: Henry Regnery), 1960.

22. Simone Weil, *Waiting for God, The Need for Roots, Gravity and Grace, First and Last Notebooks.* See *The Simone Weil Reader* ed. George Panichas (New York: Moyer Bell, 1977).

23. Teilhard de Chardin, *The Phenomenon of Man,* trans. Bernard Wall (New York: Harper and Row, 1965).

24. Teilhard de Chardin, *The Divine Milieu,* trans. by Bernard Wall (New York: Harper and Row, 1960).

25. Etienne Gilson, *The Spirit of Modern Philosophy* (Notre Dame, Ind.: University of Notre Dame Press, 1994); orig. ed. 1932, 2 vols.

26. Thomas Merton, *The Seven Story Mountain* (New York: Harcourt Brace, 1978).

27. James C. Bacik, "Contemporary Spirituality," *The New Dictionary of Catholic Spirituality* (Collegeville, Minn.: The Liturgical Press, 1993), 220.

28. Thomas Merton, *Conjectures of a Guilty Bystander* (San Francisco: Harper and Row, 1982), 517.

29. Michael Mott, *The Seven Story Mountains of Thomas Merton* (Boston: Houghton Mifflin, 1984), 311.

30. See David D. Cooper, *Thomas Merton's Act of Denial: The Evolution of a Radical Humanist* (Athens, Ga.: University of Georgia Press, 1989), 37.

31. Thomas Merton, *Contemplation in a World of Action* (London Univin, 1971), 71.

32. William D. Miller, *Dorothy Day: A Biography* (San Francisco: Harper and Row, 1982), 517.

33. See Robert McAfee Brown, *Gustavo Gutierrez: An Introduction to Liberation Theology* (New York: Orbis Books, 1990), 34.

34. Gustavo Gutierrez, *A Theology of Liberation*, trans. by Caridad Inda and John Eagleson (New York: Orbis Books, 1973).

35. See Leonardo and Clodavis Boff, *Liberation Theology* (San Francisco: Harper and Row, 1986), 17.

36. See *Hablar de Dios desde el sufrimiento del innocente* (Lima, Peru: Centro de Estudios y Publicationes (CEP), 1986, trans. by Matthew J. O'Connell as *On Job* (New York: Orbis Books, 1983), 87–88.

37. See *Beber en su proprio pozo*, (Lima, Peru: Centro de Estudios y Publicationes (CEP), 1983), trans. by Matthew J. O'Connell as *We Drink from Our Own Wells* (New York: Orbis Books, 1984), 1–3.

38. Alexander Nava, *The Mystical and Prophetic Thought of Simone Weil and Gustavo Gutierrez* (Albany, N.Y.: State University of New York Press, 2001), 81.

39. Henri Nouwen, *Reaching Out: The Three Movements of the Spiritual Life* (New York: Doubleday, 1975).

40. Jurjen Beumer, *Henri Nouwen: A Restless Seeking for God* (New York: Crossroad, 1997), 33.

41. Henri Nouwen, *Clowning in Rome: Reflections on Solitude, Celibacy, Prayer and Contemplation* (New York: Doubleday, 1979), 70.

42. Ibid., 71.

43. Ibid., 78.

44. Nouwen, *Reaching Out,* 96–97.

45. Ibid., 97.

46. Henri Nouwen, *Creative Ministry* (New York: Doubleday, 1972), 114.

47. Ibid., 115.

48. Henri Nouwen, *Life of the Beloved: Spiritual Living in a Secular World* (New York: Crossroad, 1992), 110–111.

49. Cardinal Joseph Bernardin, *The Gift of Peace: Personal Reflections* (Chicago: Loyola Press, 1997).

CHAPTER 4. LAY SPIRITUALITY AND PRAYER

1. Flannery, 397.

2. Edward C. Sellner, "Lay Spirituality," *The New Dictionary of Catholic Spirituality,* 594.

3. Flannery, 366–367.

4. Flannery, 874.

5. *Constitution on the Sacred Liturgy*, Flannery, 6.

6. Ibid., 1 and 2.

7. Eugene LaVerdiere, "Eucharistic Devotion," *The New Dictionary of Catholic Spirituality,* 360.

8. For an excellent history of the development of the sacraments, together with a pastoral analysis of the role of each sacrament in the life of Catholics today, see William J. Bausch, *A New Look at the Sacraments*, revised ed. (Mystic, Conn.: Twenty-Third Publications, 1983). Another excellent book is Bernard Cooke's *Sacraments and Sacramentality* (Mystic, Conn.: Twenty-Third Publications, 1983).

9. Edward Schillebeckx, *Christ, The Sacrament of the Encounter with God* (New York: Sheed and Ward, 1963), 3–89; see also Karl Rahner, *The Church and the Sacraments* (New York: Herder and Herder, 1966), 11–75.

10. George J. Dyer, ed. *An American Catholic Catechism* (New York: Seabury Press, 1975), 107–10.

11. Ibid., 106–7.

12. Schillebeckx, 200–16.

13. Rahner, *The Church and the Sacraments*, 41–75.

14. Karl Rahner, "Personal and Sacramental Piety," in *Theological Investigations,* trans. Karl H. Kruger (Baltimore: Helicon Press, 1963), II, 109–33.

15. Merton, *The Seven Story Mountain*, 407–423.

16. Thomas Merton, *Contemplation in a World of Action* (New York: Image Books, 1973), 186.

17. Thomas Keating, "Centering Prayer," in *The New Dictionary of Catholic Spirituality*, 139.

18. Ibid., 140.

19. Thomas Keating, *Open Mind, Open Heart: The Contemplative Dimension of the Gospel* (New York: Amity House, 1986).

20. Thomas Keating, *The Mystery of Christ: The Liturgy as Spiritual Experience* (New York: Amity House, 1987).

21. Thomas Keating, *Reawakenings* (New York: Crossroad, 1997).

CHAPTER 5. CATHOLIC FEMINIST THEOLOGY AND SPIRITUALITY

1. Catherine Mowry La Cugna, *God for Us: The Trinity and Christian Life* (San Francisco: Harper Collins, 1991), 267.

2. Anne Carr, *Transforming Grace: Christian Tradition and Women's Experience* (San Francisco: Harper Collins, 1988), 206.

3. Sandra M. Schneiders, "Feminist Spirituality," *The New Dictionary of Catholic Spirituality*, 401.

4. Carr, op. cit., 168.

5. Ibid., 169.

6. Ibid., 195.

7. Ibid.

8. Elizabeth Schussler Fiorenza, *In Memory of Her: A Feminist Theological Reconstruction of Christian Origins* (New York: Crossroad, 1983).

9. Carr, op. cit., 199.

10. McBrien, 353.

11. Elizabeth A. Johnson, *She Who Is: The Mystery of God in a Feminist Theological Discourse* (New York: Crossroad, 1992), 43–4.

12. McBrien, 354.

13. Rosemary Ruether, *Women-Church: Theology and Practice of Feminist Liturgical Committees* (San Francisco: Harper and Row, 1985), 7.

14. Flannery, 777.

15. "Justice in the World," (Washington, D.C.: United States Catholic Conference, 1971), 44.

16. Leonard Swidler and Arlene Swidler, eds. *Women Priests: A Catholic Commentary on the Vatican Declaration* (New York: Paulist Press, 1977). The text of *The Declaration on the Admission of Women to the Ministerial Priesthood*, which was published in Rome on October 15, 1976, is found in *Women Priests*, 38ff.

17. Raymond E. Brown, *Biblical Reflections on Crises Facing the Church* (New York: Paulist Press, 1975), 50, 51.

18. Tertullian, *De Cultu Feminarum*, 1:1.

19. St. Thomas Aquinas, *Summa Theologica,* I, 92, 1 and 2.

20. Ibid., III, Suppl. 65:5.

21. Brown, 57–60.

22. Flannery, 777.

23. Brown, 55.

24. Ibid., 57–60.

25. Elizabeth M. Tetlow, *Women and Ministry in the New Testament* (New York: Paulist Press, 1970), 67.

26. Raymond Brown, *Priest and Bishop* (New York: Paulist Press, 1970), 17–19.

27. Ibid., 60.

28. Quoted in Tetlow, 117.

CHAPTER 6. HISPANIC THEOLOGY AND SPIRITUALITY IN THE UNITED STATES

1. Moises Sandoval, *On the Move: A History of the Hispanic Church in the United States* (Maryknoll, N.Y.: Orbis Books, 1990).

2. Both of these letters can be obtained from the U.S. Conference of Catholic Bishops, 1312 Massachusetts Ave. N.W., Washington, D.C. 20005.

3. National Council of Catholic Bishops, "Hispanic Presence: Challenge and Commitment," in pastoral letter *On Hispanic Ministry*, 4.

4. Ibid., 5.

5. Jaffe, Ruth M. Cullen, and Thomas D. Bosnell, *The Changing Demography of Spanish Americans* (New York: Academic Press, 1980).

6. Ibid., 22.

7. Peter C. Phan, "Contemporary Theology and Inculturation in the United States," in *The Multicultural Church*, ed. William Cenker (New York: Paulist Press, 1996), 122.

8. Virgil Elizondo, *Galilean Journey: The Mexican-American Promise* (Maryknoll, N.Y.: Orbis Books, 1992). See also "Mestizaje as a Locus of Theological Reflection," in *Frontiers of Hispanic Theology in the United States*, ed. Allan Figueroa Deck (Maryknoll, N.Y.: Orbis Books, 1992), 104–23.

9. Phan, "Contemporary Theology and Inculturation," 122.

10. See Roberto Goizueto, "Theology and Intellectually Vital Inquiry: The Challenge of/to U.S. Hispanic Theologians." Proceedings of the Forty-Sixth Annual Convention of the Catholic Theological Society of America, Paul Crowley ed. (Washington, D.C.: Catholic University of America Press, 1991), 58–69.

11. German Martinez, O.S.B., "Hispanic American Spirituality," *The New Dictionary of Catholic Spirituality,* 474.

12. Ibid., 475.

13. Ibid.

14. Allan Figueroa Deck, S.J., "Proselytism and Hispanic Catholics: How Long Can We Cry Wolf?" in *America*, Dec. 10, 1988.

15. Ibid., 486.

16. Ibid., 488.

17. Ibid.

18. Ibid.

19. Ibid.

CHAPTER 7. AFRICAN-AMERICAN THEOLOGY AND SPIRITUALITY

1. *The New Dictionary of Catholic Spirituality*, 18–20.

2. Jamie T. Phelps, O.P., "Black Spirituality," in *Spiritual Traditions for the Contemporary Church*, 346.

3. *What We Have Seen and Heard* (Cincinnati, Ohio: St. Anthony Messenger Press, 1984).

4. Philips, op. cit., 342.

5. Ibid., 343.

6. William B. McClain, "American Black Worship: A Mirror of Tragedy and a Vision of Hope," in *Spiritual Traditions for the Contemporary Church*, 356.

7. W.E.B. Du Bois, *The Souls of Black Folk* (A.C.M. McClurg & Co., 1903; reprint New York: Fawcett, 1961), 380.

8. John Wesley Work, *Folk Songs of the American Negro* (New York: Howell, Soskin & Co., 1940), 87.

9. McClain, op. cit., 357.

10. *Lead Me, Guide Me: The African American Catholic Hymnal* (Chicago: G.I.A. Publications, 1987).

11. *Plenty Good Room: The Spirit and Truth of African American Catholic Worship* (Washington, D.C.: United States Catholic Conference, 1987).

12. Jay P. Dolan, 245.

13. *Brothers and Sisters To Us: U.S. Bishops Pastoral on Racism in Our Day* (Washington, D.C.: United States Catholic Conference, 1979).

14. M. Shawn Copeland, "African American Catholics and Black Theology: An Interpretation," in *African American Religious Studies,* ed. Gayraud S. Wilmore (Durham, N.C.: Duke University Press, 1989), 99–115.

15. Diana L. Hayes, "And When We Speak," in *Taking Down Our Harps*, eds. Diana L. Hayes and Cyprian Davis (Maryknoll, N.Y.: Orbis Books, 1998), 117.

16. M. Shawn Copeland, "Foundations for Catholic Theology in an African American Context," *Black and Catholic*, ed. Jamie T. Phelps, O.P. (Milwaukee, Wis.: Marquette University Press, 2nd ed., 2002), 137–39.

CHAPTER 8. DEVOTIONAL CATHOLICISM

1. Regis A. Duffy, "Devotions," *The Encyclopedia of Catholicism*, ed. Richard P. McBrien (New York: Harper Collins, 1995), 414.

2. Carl Dehne, S.J., "Devotions," *The New Dictionary of Theology*, eds. Joseph A. Komonchak, Mary Collins, and Dermot A. Las (Collegeville, Minn.: Liturgical Press, 1987), 283–88.

3. Jay P. Dolan, *In Search of an American Catholicism* (New York: Oxford University Press, 2002), 85.

4. Robert Anthony Orsi, *The Madonna of 115th Street: Faith and Community in Italian Harlem, 1880–1950* (New Haven, Conn.: Yale University Press, 1985), 4–5.

5. Dolan, 87.

6. Alan Ehrenhalt, *The Lost City: The Forgotten Virtues of Community in America* (New York: Basic Books, 1995), 120.

7. Dolan, 189.

8. Michael S. Driscoll, "Liturgy and Devotions: Back to the Future, " in *The Renewal That Awaits Us*, eds. Eleanor Bernstein, C.S.J., and Martin F. Connell (Chicago: Liturgical Training Publications, 1997), 86.

9. James Martin, S.J., ed. *Awake My Soul: Contemporary Catholics on Traditional Devotions* (Chicago: Loyola Press, 2004).

10. Flannery, "Constitution on the Sacred Liturgy," 7.

11. Congregation for Divine Worship and the Discipline of the Sacraments, *Directory on Popular Piety and the Liturgy: Principles and Guidelines* (Vatican City: 2001), no. 58.

12. Ibid., no. 1.

13. Martin, XV.

CHAPTER 9. THE CHARISMATIC MOVEMENT (RENEWAL)

1. Walter M. Abbott, ed., "Dogmatic Constitution on the Church," in *The Documents of Vatican II* (New York: America Press, 1966), 24.

2. Ibid., 559.

3. Ibid., 30.

4. Francis A. Sullivan, S.J., "The Ecclesiological Context of the Charismatic Renewal," in *The Holy Spirit and Power*, ed. Kilian McDonell, O.S.B. (Garden City, N.Y.: Doubleday, 1975), 122.

5. Léon-Joseph Cardinal Suenens, "The Charismatic Dimension of the Church," *Council Speeches of Vatican II*, ed. Yves Congar, Hans Küng, and Daniel O'Hanlon (London: Paulist Press, 1964), 18–21.

6. Abbott, 30.

7. Kilian McDonell, O.S.B., "Holy Spirit and Christian Initiation" in *The Holy Spirit and Power*, ed. Kilian McDonell, O.S.B. (Garden City, N.Y.: Doubleday, 1975), 66–67.

8. Kevin M. Ranaghan, "Liturgy and Chrisms" in *The Holy Spirit and Power*, ed. Kilian McDonell, O.S.B., 161–66; see also Richard Quebedeaux, *The New Charismatics*, II (San Francisco: Harper and Row, 1983), 72–80.

9. René Laurentin, *Catholic Pentecostalism*, trans. Matthew J. O'Connell (Garden City, N.Y.: Image Books, 1978), 73.

10. See Donald J. Gelpi, S.J., *Pentecostalism: A Theological Viewpoint* (New York: Paulist Press, 1971), 136–38.

CHAPTER 10. "SPIRITUAL" BUT NOT "RELIGIOUS"

1. Robert C. Fuller, *Spiritual but Not Religious: Understanding Unchurched America* (New York: Oxford University Press, 2001).

2. See Wade Clark Roof, *Spiritual Marketplace: Baby Boomers and the Remaking of American Religion* (Princeton, N.J.: Princeton University Press, 1999), 212.

3. Fuller, 5.

4. See Brian Zinnbauer, Kenneth Pargament, et al., "Religion and Spirituality: Unfuzzying the Fuzzy," *Journal for the Scientific Study of Religion* (December 1977), 549–64.

5. See Roof, 79–88.

6. Fuller, 98–99.

7. Ibid., 124.

8. Norman Vincent Peale, *The Power of Positive Thinking* (New York: Prentice Hall, 1952).

9. Karl Menninger, *Whatever Became of Sin?* (New York: Hawthorne Books, 1973).

10. Roy Anker, *Self-Help and Popular Religion in Early American Culture* (Westport, Conn.: Greewood Press, 1999), 119.

11. Wuthnow, op. cit., 3.

12. Roof, 121.

Index